love like a
son-of-a-bitch

juan vargas

DonJuanVargas.com

ISBN-13: 978-1481967181
ISBN-10: 1481967185

For everyone.

table of contents

mushroom power

How we're doing it, we're doing it wrong, it seems to me. And it seems that I'm not the only one to think that way. It is not a pessimistic attitude: all the historic accounts would make us think that we are a violent species. Our history is prolific in envy, egoism, hate, forms of domestic violence, wars, territorial disputes, massacres, murders, rape, kidnappings, concentration camps, and a varied spectrum of other aggressions.

While it is true that aggression is a characteristic present in nature, only us, human beings, have the tools to translate it into violent acts that surpass the universe's fair play limits. These, despite the fact of not being written, discard bombings, biological arms and tortures, and they do not justify, for example, the existence of a market for movies where human beings are raped and mutilated live: snuff movies.

I think it is unnecessary to continue explaining to what aspect of our behaviour I am referring to, because even if there is someone plainly satisfied with our society, that someone cannot deny the atrocities that go on.

Our violence and its acceptance reach such a level that in the past an apocalyptic ending to our

ignorance was predicted. Today, we believe sub-
missively that we are living the evidence that proves
it. A more pathetic attitude cannot be found in the
*Archaeological Museum of Extinct Species of the Uni-
verse...*

To top off this auto-destructive attitude, the
human species has embarked itself into an inefficient economic system that has resulted in a society
where absolutely everything is monetised, alienating
us from any activity that does not have an economic
value. If one day we were a predominant species on
planet Earth, today we live subjugated and used in
the *Kingdom of Money.*

The progressive loss of love in our society is
also evident when we consider the damage that we
are causing to other species and ecosystems of our
Mother Earth. But more painful than seeing how
we are abusing our beautiful little planet, is how we
justify ourselves and do not make the effort to stop
our harmful practices.

In this restless development in which we have
engaged since time unknown, the most important el-
ements of existence have been replaced progressively. Love and the family nucleus have been substituted by a selfish and cold individualism. Dreams and
imagination are being lost in a strict logical system,
which only serves to homogenise thought, castrating
any outburst of creativity. Trusting peers and feeling responsible for each other is unthinkable today.

And enjoying small things, which are the particles that compose life—eating, copulating, sleeping, breathing, etc.—have been eclipsed by stupid tasks and responsibilities that seek to sustain an economic system more than the pursuit of an individual's fulfilment.

The only defence in favour of the Western Civilisation's current state—that nowadays includes the entire human race, with the exception of a few bubbles that are about to be absorbed, or are involved in a teleological struggle that has not coined an explicit and feasible alternative to the West—are economic development and technological advances. The first pretends, erratically, to be a measurement of the quality of life, but only manages to strengthen the economic empires and the welfare of the few who are touched by the power of money. The second one is over-dimensioned to make us believe that the path we are taking now is the best there is. There is even a fraction of the scientific community that is so dull as to believe that the great discoveries and inventions left to be made could be counted with the fingers of your hand.

determination to improve

All right, enough of weeping, for this book is not a reminder of our pathetic situation. This book is an indecent proposal. The world is in crisis, so I guess we just have to reinvent it, to dream it all over again.

History has taught us that civilisations are born, have an apogee phase and then they decay. The West seems to be in this latter phase. It is not my intention to deny the advances of the West, but it is time for a change. We are stuck culturally, and the only way to reactivate our potential and imagination is to follow a different path. Even if we are in a dead-end now, we have the foundation that may precede a powerful civilisation developed up to be a space civilisation. It is a matter of not getting attached blindly to the current model, and of not drowning possibilities of development that are more efficient.

The transition between a decaying and an emerging civilisation generally includes violence and conflicts. However, I believe that our species has the ability to avoid that unnecessary tradition—it is yet to be seen if we have the guts to do it. And here is where this proposal comes in. What I intend with this book is to lay out an experiment that would make such a transition—between the Western Civilisation and the following one, whatever it may be—in an efficient, easy to apply, non violent and fun way.

The experiment is based on creating a type of society that is more efficient than the West in its economic system and its socio-political organisation, which correspond to the second and third chapter, respectively. The need to find a superior scientific and technologic path can be derived, too, which will be discussed in the fourth chapter. Also, we will require some changes in our interpersonal behaviour, and our mental and educational development, which is the topic of the fifth chapter. The last chapter elaborates more on the experiment.

Consciously creating a new civilisation is something ambitious, but not because of that impossible or complicated. Creating a better society can also sound relative, because we enter into a definition that is absolutely subjective. But in order to avoid getting into that topic, which would be useless at this point, I take three points as the experiment's objectives: to create a society that enjoys absolute peace and love; to develop all human activities without deteriorating the environment in the least; and, as a point of reference with the West in the development field, to leave it behind rapidly in the space race.

I choose this last objective because, besides it being my dream since a very early age—and I am sure that many people share this dream—I believe that travelling through space is representative of an optimal development. To become a space civilisation it is not enough to develop an advanced propulsion technology. In order to become one, we will have to develop the entire spectrum of sciences; create a harmonious society; and be efficient in the management of our natural resources, as well as in the use of human potential. It is stupid to believe that intergalactic trips can be made while we are killing each other down here and are destroying the planet.

mushroom metaphor

After sketching the content of this book and having defined some reference points, there is only left for me to explain the title of this chapter: mushroom power.

The only thing that is stopping us from really developing, and enjoying life, love, peace and nature; is fear. We are afraid of disposing of the pillars of our society, of the unknown, of risking everything and dedicating ourselves to enjoy life; we are afraid that perfection exists, to arrive at a point where all our perspectives are positive.

Fear is our greatest predator. It starts by making us underestimate our capacity to dream and imagine. Then, we end up shitting in our pants; holding tight to some rules that we invented and that, illusively, we call reality. At a very early age we begin to forget that everything is possible and magical. We should never stop being children; it is not necessary to mature so much. Not if we are going to live for the rest of our lives afraid of being free to the point of defining our own future.

Here is where the mushroom metaphor comes in. Of all the organisms, the mushroom is the one that I admire the most (actually, the mushroom is only the fruit of fungus, which are rather complex organisms that add up to a large number of species, but for simplicity's sake, I will refer to them as mushrooms). They grow in decomposing organisms, excrements, and in any place and under any circumstance that you would consider impossible to support life. It is precisely that will to live, that determination to fight, that I want us to copy. Analogously, if our society is a mess, we have to blossom to create a powerful and loving civilisation.

The experiment that I propose is not difficult to achieve, but it will only be possible if in our blood runs that power that stops at nothing, and that magic that knows no impossible. Characteristics that made our evolution possible, but that currently I see reduced in our species. I feel that our only engine today is that of obtaining money, as if it were the air that makes our existence possible. But the power to imagine, to dream and to fight for these dreams are dissolving progressively in a conformist society that tends to homogenise everything.

Mushroom power, an overdose of the will to live, is what we need to change the terrible and mediocre image described at the beginning of this chapter. If we want a better world we have to move. By crying and supposing we are not going to change it, neither by waiting for a pissed off god to come down to put the planet into order. Life is what we want it to be; but we only have one, and we have it now. If we want life to be a dream of happiness and love, we have to fight until we achieve that. The word *utopia* was coined by an impotent man...

It is convenient to explain what I mean by fighting. Even if the concept that I have of the West is that of a tired and decadent society, and I want to

propose an alternative to it, I do not do it from a re-
sented and hateful stand. There are those who think
that the best deeds are made in moments of desper-
ation, fury and depression. I don't, I think that the
best deeds are made after a good orgasm. With this
I pretend to illustrate that, in order to create a better
civilisation, we have to start with a devouring enthu-
siasm, not with a fundamentalist resentment. More
than destroying or fighting against the West, we have
to trace another path. And we have to do it with love
and a lot of laughter. Otherwise, we might trace another path, but it will lead us to the same shit.

Finally, I must clarify that the ideas, stands and
practices proposed in this book are not definitive or
dogmatic. It will be during the planning and, mainly, during the execution of the experiment where
they will be defined. Maybe I should write this book
in 20 or 30 years so that I could elaborate more in
its content. But I am not trying to write a good book,
I am trying to launch a magnificent and fun project.

Any suggestions, complements or contradic-
tions to my proposal are welcome. The objective of
this book, that is more a working document, is precisely to obtain the help of those who want to stop
crying and really do something. Mushroom power!

from economy to ecosystems

The first step to prepare the terrain where a superior civilisation would grow is to reconsider the current economic system. The Western model implies certain inefficiencies and complications that are slowing down our development. Differences may be found regarding this point, because some people believe that buildings, highways and more money are representative of development. But if we keep in mind that the objective is to become a space civilisation, money in itself is not very helpful unless we use it as fuel.

At this point of our evolution as a species with a high social organisation, restructuring our economy is vital. If in the past the transition between two periods was often accompanied by an economic adjustment, now we have to be more radical and conscious of the changes we must make in order to attain a greater efficiency.

The difference between the past and today is that never before had a civilisation rotated around money and its economic activities. Without entering into ethical judgements, it can be said that the economy takes priority in our society. Architecture is a good measurement in this sense. For many cultures their obsession was the afterlife, god or the defence of their territories—that is why we see pyramids in Egypt, cathedrals in Europe and a wall in China. Today, business centres take the shape of skyscrapers to show their power and our dedication to money.

This cult could be valid like any other. But the implications it has on the environment, society and the individual are making our development take an unnecessary detour.

In order to develop deeply we have to change our priority: from economy to ecosystems. And in order for this to be possible, it is necessary to start from an ecosystemic ground and derive from there the human economy.

earth is an organism

It is time to begin understanding life as something more integral. Life is not an organism or a species, but a force that represents itself in different forms. From atoms—going through molecules, genes, cells, organs, organisms, species, ecosystems, planets, solar systems, star clusters, galaxies and galaxy clusters—to the universe as a whole, everything is alive, and everything fights to survive and to perpetuate life. The limit of our organism is not our skin, and our survival depends directly on our relation with other people, species and the small planet on which we live. We are part of a complex life system.

We define organism as an entity that is born, grows and/or develops, reproduces and dies. Likewise, the cells in our body are born, grow and/or develop, reproduce and die. Are our cells organisms within our bodies? Yes; they are life forms within another. Human beings and all the other organisms that inhabit this planet are born, grow and/or develop, reproduce and die. Analogously, we are "cells" in this organism that we call Mother Earth. Earth is an organism; a living being; a superior life form than ours. By superior I do not mean it is better or more important, but that it comprehends a greater level of complexity. Life is only one in the entire universe, where the only priority is for life to continue, no matter how it manifests itself.

If your cells suddenly had the reasoning that we have—it is not that cells lack reason, but that it is different from ours, and their perception of the universe is different—how could they know that they are part of your body? What evidence would they need to accept that they are part of a superior organism? Apparently, it is impossible, unless they understood what their function in your body was. Perhaps they could develop sciences and technologies; one day they could even build a "space ship;" go out of your body; take pictures of it; and return jubilant. Your cells would probably think that the universe is a peculiar space; with "planets" that have the shape of your contour, and the contour of the other species that inhabit Earth. Only if your cells knew that their survival needs and their natural impulses respond to some vital functions to you, they would understand that they are cells in your body. How would you explain to one of your red-blood cells that it is a red-blood cell and not the centre of the universe? How would you convince it to treat you carefully?

But you do not have to accept that Earth is an organism. Even if I believe that, it is not my intention to convince you of it. I describe it simply because I think it is a useful metaphor to understand the interrelation level in which the life of our species evolves. Also, it seems to me that this perspective can help us to relate more lovingly to our surroundings, which is a first order requirement for a proper natural resources management. More than living in a habitat, we have to co-live. Co-living among us, with our planet, and later on with the universe.

Here I have to give some credit to the West because, every day, more people are understanding our relationship with the environment. We experience this so much today, that even multinationals—accused of being the main polluters—include in their agendas the pursuit of ecological efficiency. If this process does not go as fast as we wish, it is not only because we are lacking a strict institutional determination, but because consumers themselves (us) function in this inefficient system. Example: we attack oil companies, but we all drive cars and demand petroleum derivatives in large quantities.

The West has begun to develop an ecological conscience that with some sacrifice can evolve into an efficient society, we are progressively beginning to understand that biodiversity—understood as biomass or as the number of species—plays a primary role in the conservation of ecosystems in the long run; and our survival depends directly on this. We have to be careful not to protect biodiversity only because it represents a source of capital, as it is customary to do nowadays.

Despite our progressive ecological consciousness, our economic activities continue to hurt the planet. In our precarious understanding of Earth and its biotic mechanisms, we have come to the conclusion that many species die and are born everyday. The life span of a species is as of today unpredictable, but the human process of systematic and industrial predatory practices is imposing a rhythm superior to that which ecosystems can take. An ice age implies a reduction in the biodiversity but it does not appear in a few years. During the last few centuries we have modified radically the appearance of the majority of the ecosystems of our little planet, and we have done it in such a way that we have reduced the biodiversity.

In order to mend this ecosystemic damage we have to start accepting that we are just another animal that inhabits Earth. Despite the development and peculiarities of humans, we are just another species among the millions that live in our Mother Earth. Life in this planet does not adjust to our survival. In the same way that we emerged, we can go extinct.

We justify the current biodiversity degradation that we are causing by the increasing demand that our development implies. We take resources from the planet because, like any other species, we are determined to survive. But the way in which we do it is given by our species' characteristics: a superior mammal that has adapted to almost all terrestrial ecosystems of the planet, and at the same time has developed considerable capacities to reason and imagine.

In the evolution race we have relied on these jokers, and thus, starting with the hominids, the fight for survival on planet Earth has included organisms that have the capacity to shape their surroundings and make sophisticated tools. There is nothing twisted so far: we have only tried to extend our existence as a species, which is written in capital letters in our genetic code. However, if we take into account the ecological destruction that we are causing, we should stop, re-evaluate and restate our stand in the evolution race.

Our stay on the planet and the possibility to expand throughout space depends on our adaptation and efficient relationship with the habitat where we live—first here on Earth, and then in any corner of the universe. The current economic system has not reached a level of efficiency in our interaction with the ecosystems, and that is why it requires an urgent restructuring.

current human economy

Prior to explaining the necessary changes in Western society, in order to become an ecologically efficient society that accomplishes technological advances superior to the ones available today, we must reformulate the concept of economy. Economy is commonly defined as the science that studies the allocation and management of resources for the production of goods and services that a society demands. Capital, raw materials and labour are understood by resources.

Capital, money, is a concept that in the past three millenniums has facilitated the exchange of products and the accumulation of goods. As human societies increased in size and organised in more complex structures, the need to exchange goods in order to guarantee the sustenance of the population arose. In the beginning this exchange was done directly: one thing for another. But in order for this trade to occur, the demands and supplies of both parties had to match. Something that was always handy were metals. That is why they served as a bridge for exchange, because somebody could give something in exchange for a metal to exchange it later on for anything that he needed. Thus emerged coins, which had a real value: their weight. With time, the exponential increase of trade generalised the use of coins.

Another obvious advantage of money was its capacity to accumulate. If somebody had a surplus of his land's production he would loose it, for the majority of products perish. This inconvenience was overcome with money, and the accumulation of goods through time became possible. The discovery of the Americas, the Industrial Revolution and the creation of the bank (and consequently, credit) made the agricultural economy pass to a secondary stage, and was substituted by an industrial capitalist economy. Money then formed the basis for a society focused on the production and consumption of goods.

The strengthening of industry and new production technologies, that resulted in line production, meant an ever increasing demand for resources. Furthermore, marketing and advertising techniques have made the American Dream spread out in our society like a cancer. Today, the West is almost a global civilisation that transpires its idolatry for consumption; that does not stop to consider the implications that its practices of resource extraction practices might have on future generations.

That's how we live working under the orders of money. But the first step towards the empire of money was taken long before and perhaps coincided with the commercialisation of sex. Today, prostitution is

the lesser illness in a society that measures everything in terms of money, from death to life—currently, organisms can be patented in many countries.
The only thing that we cannot really commercialise
today is love. But if we continue in this capitalist
society I am sure that, in some twisted manner, we
will be capable of taking that last step and become
the perfect whores...

Our demand for raw materials has meant a loss
of ecosystems that only our species can brag about
having caused. In our historical knowledge, no other species has been so hazardous and destructive.
Despite knowing that we are contaminating, industrial activities stand as an immovable priority of our
society.

Human beings have managed to maintain a
linear economic development in the last millennia
(although when money is scarce we panic and call
it a recession) because our population growth has
only exploded in the last two centuries. But the future will not be so agreeable if we do not change our
development; and if we continue to diminish life on
this planet while our population and demand for resources continue to grow.

On the other hand, the labour force, the work
of humans, is just another variable in the chain
production. Phenomena such as unemployment
or the exploitation of workers have been assumed
as externalities of the capitalist system. If communism introduced a restatement on the importance of

workers—that resulted in an improvement of working conditions—neither the communist theory nor its applications present an alternative to the society we live in. Communism is just the other side of the capitalist coin; the dispute is on who should have the coin.

We have conformed a society whose final objective is economic development through capital and industry. If aliens made a report on our society, money would certainly be our cornerstone. The objective today is to attain a certain economic level, that allows us to do all other activities. Things so elemental to a species such as enjoying life (whatever this may mean), eating, having a child, education, travelling, etc., are determined by the economic level of each individual.

Western society, addicted to consumption more and more, seems to kneel before money. The trend today is the consolidation of giant multinationals which, if we continue the way we are, will galvanise and control all aspects of our society. The importance of the state is being taken over by the multinationals, which are the ones who generate capital. People start to talk about a neo-feudalism, where the lords are the multinationals; and the servants, all those who do not have a good job.

I must clarify that multinationals are no more than a human product. Judging them or those who control them would not be fair, because as I said before, all of us participate in this economic system that we have created. Multinationals are just another actor in the polar structure that we inherited from our ancestors—where by definition there are actors with power and others without. These positions of power were taken before by rulers or religious leaders. We must modify this hierarchical system; but finding a solution does not consist in blaming, but in understanding that the problem is something structural.

In short, our economy—that is, the relation with the ecosystems of our planet—is projected exclusively from an anthropocentric point. The ecological variables have only begun to gain importance in the last three decades, and they are not relevant enough as to restrict those activities that damage—or may damage—the ecosystems where we live.

ecosystems

To obtain an ecological efficiency we must cross out the definition of economy, and redefine it as part of a more complex discipline: ecosystems. Human economy is just a fraction of the ecosystems, and inversely, ecosystems are the sum of the economies of many species. All the species have an economy that is based in the extraction of resources, helping maintain those resources, and returning useful residue to the ecosystem; and this economy is always interrelated to the economies of other species.

Symbiotic relationships are a constant in nature, we could not live on our own. Life is only one.

The mother principle of efficiency is the respect for the economies of other species, a respect where giving and taking are proportional. The efficiency consists in integrating with the ecosystem and operating within it according to its own mechanisms, not in adapting it exclusively to our needs.

Our anthropocentric vision has resulted in only considering human needs in our economic analysis, and in regarding natural resources as linear inputs whose lives begin when they are taken; go through manufacture, sales and purchase; and conclude when their use expires. This is a mistake that must be corrected at once. We are a species that does not understand that resources must be looked after, that we must be synchronised with the planet's mechanisms of life regeneration.

If suddenly some bacteria decided that they needed to consume all the oxygen in the planet to develop certain infrastructure and industries that would allow them to accumulate capital, we would certainly think that they should eat a lot of shit. We do the same thing with many resources and are drowning the economies of other species. Please! It's like telling children to share their toys: the planet belongs to everyone.

The changes that we must make to redirect us ecologically will have radical repercussions in our society. But we must not be afraid of change, it is natural to stop and re-evaluate our activities at certain points of our evolution.

The starting point of an economic restatement is finding a sustainable development. Sustainable means that the ecosystemic management also guarantees the subsistence of the other species—and thus, that of our future generations—in such a manner that the extinction of a species or an ecosystemic change only occurs due to intrinsic factors of Earth or of her space surroundings.

Development means a progressive improvement in the quality of life. It is of utmost importance to understand that the quality of life is given by our perception and use of some material variables (environmental quality, food, shelter and some utensils) and other intangible ones (love, education, entertainment, peace and health). Nowadays, economic analyses do not take into account environmental quality, love and peace—because they are not quantifiable; and health, education and food are quantified without caring about the quality, the benefit or the fun that come with them. In a new economic system we must consider that love, having pure air, living without the annoying violence, etc., are more important than the amount of TV sets or cars that the inhabitants of a region may have. Having them in excess is not only inefficient for the ecosystem, but usually it does not represent a latent improvement in the quality of life. We should concentrate first in the "small things" that make us enjoy life, and then build those that we need to progress.

Economists have always been characterised for supposing too much, but it is time for economics to turn into an empirical science. Economists, who should not see in these ideas a ticket to unemployment, must become planners of our necessities, the resources available, and how these two can meet. They cannot be just model crafters. And working with needs and resources as a unique concept should be done at community and regional levels, not at national or global ones. Thus, ecology should override economics.

Ecological efficiency consists in letting the natural mechanisms of the ecosystem operate freely. In this way we would also minimise our effort to obtain the resources that we need.

money

The first step to attain a sustainable development is to abolish money. Money is a human invention; not a natural element for survival. If other species can live without it, we can, too. We are not inferior to not be able to do it, nor superior to insist on its important benefit.

It is imperative to abolish money because it represents a subjective human value that cannot evaluate representatively other organisms or their needs. We cannot continue to monetise life according to our convenience. Life does not have a price, and assigning one prostitutes it.

A society without money does not accumulate: it has an optimal management of resources. Accumulation implies that we produce more than we need in a given period of time. In other words, we use up more resources than we need, which represents less resources for future generations, and a present need to increase artificially the production of those resources.

Besides the power struggle that money implies—which translates into violence, wars and the rupture of family and social nucleus—money causes another inefficiency in our civilisation: it alienates us from the utility of work and things. Our society works for money, not for what it needs. For example, by not working directly in obtaining our food, we do not appreciate it as such, but the money that buys it. It is not the utility of things, but obtaining and having what moves us. We work a lot but we do not enjoy what we have; therefore cats consider us the most imbecile creatures on the planet—and they are not mistaken.

Hilarious as it may sound, the denominator of our society should be love and not money. Now: the models, projections and graphs that economists love to do so much would be obsolete, for love is not quantifiable. But neither is it necessary to have a mathematical formula to tell us if we are progressing or not. What matters is that we feel better and that we leave our children a better society than the one we received. There is more money all the time in the world's monetary system and a greater number of products available to the consumer, but any parent would have to agree with me that the society we are leaving our children is not necessarily better. If you do not believe me, spend an entire day with them.

Perhaps economists, and political and industrial leaders would say that it is impossible to say farewell to money. It is not. Perhaps some would say that we do not have to be so radical, that we could develop a mixed system. Money is or is not, but it does not negotiate. It's like pregnancy: either you are or you are not, but you can't be a little pregnant.

Abolishing money could cause a social chaos. To that, all I can say is that we must take the crash as it comes: sometimes in life one's got to have balls. It is part of our responsibility to take the consequences of correcting an acute error that hurts all life forms on this planet. We must abolish money; and we cannot do it in a progressive manner: the mechanisms in charge of keeping the cohesion and perpetuation of a system do not allow its basis to be modified, and money is the basis of the Western Civilisation.

No matter how painful it turns out to be to abandon money, we cannot allow it to continue causing havoc in our society and in our Mother Earth. Perhaps money has some benefits, but its negative implications reach such magnitude that we cannot hesitate. What is the worst thing that can happen to us if we discard money? I am sure that the consequences will be no worse than what we see around us.

To all those who cannot conceive a world without money, I remind you that things are not made with money but with work.

autosufficiency

The lack of money presents a radical impediment on trade because a barter system is not efficient at exchanging products in an open global market. This will preoccupy many economists, politicians and multinationals. I am sorry, but precisely, there should not be any trade. Contrary to the idea that efficiency is attained by a global market—where resources are distributed perfectly, production is maximised, and costs are minimised, because one benefits from the comparative advantages of each region—commerce is inefficient and is only useful to feed an anthropocentric capitalist system where environmental preservation is not a priority.

Trade implies an over-exploitation of the ecosystem because more resources are extracted in order to export them, and it implies a greater pollution by increasing production and by transporting those goods. Trade also demands a greater demand for energy. The production of energy, from coal plants to nuclear reactors, is one of the human activities that generates more pollution.

Abolishing trade necessarily raises the question of how we are going to get what we need. Thus, each community should produce everything it needs using the resources that its ecosystem offers. To do this we will have to concentrate on learning to produce all that we want, but only with the resources present in our ecosystem. Most likely this production system will present a lesser number of products to chose from and a slower rhythm of production than a capitalist system. If it takes longer it is because we are slow to learn; because our limitation of resources requires a technological innovation in terms of materials; or simply because one has to wait a little longer. No big deal. The consumption rush has made us believe that we got to have everything instantly. If we have to wait and not have the thousand products that a capitalist market economy offers, we wait and that is all. Managing resources in a sustainable and responsible way is more important than being able to accumulate things.

We have to develop an autosufficiency in all the regions of the world. Each community must produce what it needs, each ecosystem must be preserved to produce the resources required by the community and the species that inhabit it—the area of autosufficiency should be given by the characteristics of the ecosystem. That is efficiency at its best.

An autosufficiency in resources should also be accompanied by a reciprocal extraction of resources: we will have to give to the ecosystem in the same intensity that we take from it; and to make sure that what we give is required by the ecosystem—otherwise it is pollution. Our natural residue (organic wastes, carbon, matter, energy, etc..) are raw materials for the ecosystem; they are recycled by other life forms and used as their sustenance. On the other hand, toxic, nuclear and some solid wastes are lethal for the ecosystems of Earth, and there does not exist any justification to continue producing them. Attempts such as reducing carbon emissions into the atmosphere, controlling nuclear waste disposal and recycling synthetic materials are a noble act of faith, but they are insufficient. We must be more radical and abolish any activity that damages the ecosystem or any other species.

Our economic analyses have never included an honest evaluation of the importance of preserving an ecosystemic equilibrium. We consider the maximisation of production, but not the return of our wastes—our contribution to the planet. The USA is considered the greatest economic power by account of its industrial production. However, it is the country that holds the greatest indexes of garbage disposal and energy consumption per capita. We are seriously mistaken. Efficiency consists in not unlinking the taking of resources from the production of wastes—which in ecosystemic relations are the same thing—and it is obtained by minimising the resources extracted and making sure that the wastes are absorbed immediately by the ecosystem.

labour

Another advantage of a non-monetary system is that unemployment is eliminated. The unemployment that the Western Civilisation presents is accounted for the fact that we work for money, and when it is scarce, work also is—the old unemployment and inflation paradigm. But by definition there cannot be unemployment, because nobody is useless and we can all do an activity that benefits our community.

The solution is that we all work in food production, education and in something that we like. We would all work in food production, processing and preparation because we are animals and we all need to eat. There cannot be any parasites in a species as creative and restless as the human species. The idea of task specialisation does not exclude anybody from doing the only thing he needs to do to survive: get food.

Taking care and educating children—which we have been doing pretty badly—should be a social labour to reinforce better some values such as love and respect. If the objective is to live peacefully in society, participating directly in the teaching of the fundamentals that make it possible is everybody's business. On the other hand, we all have something that we want to learn and something that we can teach others. Education is a determinant that improves the quality of life as it helps towards the fulfilment of the individual, and in the system proposed here it will allow us to produce the things we need.

After dedicating time to food production and education (both teaching and learning), each individual would have to work on something of his vocation— here is where work specialisation comes in. We all have a vocation, but in the current system we cannot always do what we want because we have to work to gain our sustenance. This results in an inefficient waste of the potential that each one of us has inside. How many more artists, scientists or athletes we would have if money was not a necessity?

agriculture

The Western agricultural industry is notorious because, in the rush for increasing productivity indexes, we complicate ourselves too much and we interrupt the natural mechanisms of ecosystem regeneration. Nowadays, to obtain an agricultural product we need improved seeds, fertilisers, herbicides, plaguicides and preservatives, among others.

Nevertheless, we cannot forget that the objective of agriculture is to feed the human population, which we are not achieving. Agricultural technology exists, but hunger and malnutrition continue among us because the mechanisms of food distribution and sales continue to be the same. Eradicating hunger is not a technological matter, but a structural one.

The alimentary problem of the world cannot be unlinked from factors such as overpopulation;

erosion caused by non-ecological agricultural practices; not having money to use the costly and anti-ecological inputs that Western agriculture requires; the inefficient demographic distribution of our species; and our alimentary habits that are characterised by a poor diet.

These factors translate into an inefficient management of resources that make impossible to eradicate hunger and malnutrition. Eradicating them is perhaps the greatest challenge that we have to face, because even if we continue to be the centre of the universe, we still need to eat. Unfortunately for our interests, we cannot feed on our own ego. Thus, the most viable path to supply our alimentary needs is a return to a local agricultural economy. It is important to get rid of the idea that an agricultural society implies a scientific and technological deceleration.

In the past years, natural agricultural practices have begun to gain importance in the scientific spheres, and in some consumer and production sectors. This is due to the fact that traditional agriculture, although it does not present the same productivity indexes as the technical one, represents a lesser environmental impact and implies a more balanced diet: the farmer or traditional grower works with a greater number of species than an industrial producer.

The environment gives us the food that we need; we only have to make sure that we do not obstruct the natural regeneration mechanisms of the ecosystems and of not abusing extraction practices. Surviving is not complicated: evidence for this is that all the species that live with us do so. Our industrial and creative characteristics should not be expressed in an unleashed agricultural production, but in an understanding and natural management of the habitat that would allow us to supply our alimentary demand.

Restructuring the agricultural sector must be thought at a small scale; at a community level and in a manner that it involves all the members of the community. We would have to retake the ancestral and traditional knowledge on the management of resources that, as well as the soil, is eroding more and more everyday. We would also have to develop adequate agricultural technology. Finally, and what is more complicated for us, we would have to *share* seeds and agricultural knowledge.

industrial production

Nowadays, the industrial production trend is towards multinationals, which are no more than monopolies with a supra-government power. The economic race has given a green light to any type of industry, with the sole objective of generating more capital. That is how industrial capitalism galvanises today our society and makes us produce an infinity of products that are unnecessary. When companies enter a competition to occupy a greater part of the market, an irresponsible extraction of resources

that hurts the environment is generated. The commercialisation of products is adjusted to marketing
strategies that aim at maximising our consumption.
The production of goods in our civilisation is an objective in itself; not a medium to satisfy our needs.

In a society without money, that does not trade
and where everyone works in the food sector, an obvious question arises: How are clothes, tools, basic
utensils and the required machines made? We have
to go back to crafty methods of production. Bye-bye
to industrial production. Here it is convenient to
clarify that technological goods can also be produced
in a crafty way.

My first argument for the farewell party for the
industrial revolution is a matter of aesthetics. Who
could deny that the most beautiful things are those
hand made, such as a Rolls Royce and a Stradivar-
ius? With our hands we give life and love to things,
a gift that cannot be emulated by line production
robots.

Another advantage of craft production is its
ecological efficiency. Craft production is directed to
supply the needs of a community, not to increase
sales and conquest the global market, so resource
extraction is a lot less. If the materials used come
from the same ecosystem, these will be biodegradable to a greater extent than what we see today.
Also, not having trade will mean that packaging
will be obsolete, which in itself represents a great

deal of contamination, both at production and the disposal phases.

The quality of the products is also a latent benefit. Generally, hand made products have a better quality because their production is evaluated at each step. On the other hand, without a commercial engine and relaying on an adequate information system, the products developed will be upgraded more easily. Most likely, things that are already obsolete at the time of production will not be produced: today, they sell us "state-of-the-art" technology that in fact was available a few years ago, but that they need to commercialise now to recover the investment, and thus in the future sell us products that are already developed but that it is not convenient to commercialise today.

Finally, an industrial reduction implies a brutal decrease in the demand for electricity, which is an industrial sector in itself, and very important for both its generation of capital and for the environmental degradation that it causes.

A crafty production system—that would not imply a lesser quality of life than the one offered by a capitalist industrial society—is only possible if there is a knowledge exchange among the communities, a good education and if the verb *to give* is conjugated by all the members of our society. Within a community there will emerge labour specialisation, not as something forced but as a mediation process between the needs (determined culturally) of that community, and the inclination of each individual. The secret to this type of society consists in each individual doing what he likes, and that he shares it with others.

transition from economy to ecosystems

In the last section, I sketched some steps to follow in order to restructure the current economic system: abolish money and trade; reach an auto-sufficiency in all the resources and an ecosystemic equilibrium; and reform the agricultural and industrial sectors.

Does it appear too simplistic? It is. In fact, I am absolutely convinced that everything in the world is not only possible but also easy. If something is not, it is because we are doing it wrong. Thus, we have to look for the way to make it well, easy.

Explaining the specific procedure to make the transition from a human economy to an ecologically efficient society would be to underestimate the liberty and creativity of my fellow human beings. To a same problem, each region, each ethnic group, each community can (and should) react satisfactorily but yet in a different fashion. Describing in detail that process would be pedantic or the job of a fortune-teller, which I'm not. I only want to emphasise that this sort of change is possible and easy, and I want to invite you to give it a try.

The only thing that I can detail of the transition phase is that releasing from our shoulders the weight that money represents, we would be able to enjoy other values that life has. For example, love, that never devaluates.

Today, we are working too hard to increase productivity and capital, but the quality of life does not present a latent improvement. And to complement this, fun is not our priority—perhaps this sounds too banal, but I just cannot understand why we are a species for which work is more important than enjoying life. Could it be that it is because we are the most imbecile?

The problems that the Western Civilisation presents are latent and we cannot wait for the future generations to solve them. It has to be us who channel our species into a pacifist, efficient and fun development path, or do you have something better to do? The only thing that is required from us is to have no fear. The consequences do not matter, afterwards we will think how to solve the problems that may arise, but now we have to detach ourselves from material things, which hurt life so much on this beautiful and playful little planet. If our ancestors survived the ice ages, we can survive without money.

socio-political organisation

A space civilisation is incubated in an atmosphere free from the pressure imposed by the internal competition for money and power. The current socio-political organisation implies many flaws that are justified as side effects of the system or human imperfections when adapting a perfect model. Both excuses are inadmissible, because the function of a society is to benefit its members—and to do that it must do whatever is necessary.

Since the objective of the experiment is to make a peaceful and quick transition between two civilisations, parallel to an economic reform we must restructure our socio-political organisation. It is convenient to clarify here that by talking of a new civilisation I do not want to be pretentious. It is simply the obvious consequence of abolishing the Western Civilisation's basis: money, the state and anthropocentrism.

I believe that we (humans) have attained such a level of intelligence and we have such a capacity to love, that we can make the transition between civilisations not be the product of a painful struggle for power—how it has been customary for our species.

I trust in our generation to set up a precedent by detaching ourselves from power to evolve peacefully. That would be the most important legacy that we could leave our descendants.

Our socio-political organisation must direct itself to generate a much superior society than ours. To do this we must eliminate the cast structure and the flawed idea that power should be concentrated; while we create a society that motivates and promotes the capacities of each individual.

power game

The power struggle that exists among the different species and within a single species is recurrent in nature. However, in human beings the internal struggle has stopped being a survival mechanism. Our power rush is motivated by demonstrating the supremacy of the individual; it is an objective in itself.

If we are a social animal it is because we obtain certain benefits from living in a society. Mainly: love, knowledge and a sense of protection. Then, to live peacefully in society we would have to balance the personal interests with those of the community—these latter imply by definition a benefit for the individual. We must not encourage social interests when these hide those of a few people, which has been reiterative in our history.

Money is not the only mechanism in our society to accumulate power, although it is the most versatile. There is also political power, that is the one we give an individual or an institution to govern us. The economic and political power complement each other and operate according to the same game rules. Therefore, by developing a society without money, a void will be created, which will make necessary a socio-political restructure.

To establish a new type of society we must simplify the individual-society relationship, and attach it to concrete objectives. Politics, as well as economics, has turned into an abstract and theoretical field. We accept this condition pathetically, forgetting that our needs are real. This is what in game theory is known as coprosystem: some talk shit and the others eat it.

It is convenient to clarify here that if I propose to end with power, I am referring to the institutional one, not the one that is inherent to each individual. We must encourage the power that is not obtained by taking away that of others or by institutional mechanisms; I am talking about the power of the individual as a living being that fights to demonstrate that he is alive.

trayectory

Human beings, like many other organisms, at some point of our evolution began to group to look for an evolutionary advantage. The way of grouping has evolved constantly and in each country or region it has had different characteristics and length. In this section I will describe superficially the trajectory of our power struggle—that has passed from autocracy, aristocracy and concluded in democracy, the fashion of the moment—in order to shed some light in what a path to follow could be.

As the population in the communities increased, the organisation of its members became more complex, and specialisation emerged. Dividing the work implied a structure that was able to delegate and supervise at the same time: a hierarchy. An equivalent example is the organisation seen in ants or bees.

And in the same manner that happens with our brother insects, a vacant at the top of the pyramid arose in the human structure. In the beginning, probably the law of the strongest was true, which evolved into the figure of the emperor, religious leader or monarch; arguing that the power was theirs in account for their sagacity, divine order or succession, respectively. Independently of the mode, the concentration of power in a leader (autocracy) was the same; the responsibility of guiding a community was put in the hands of an individual.

But the continuous increase of the population, the diversification of human activities and the lack of conformism of a few, made it necessary to delegate some power. The first beneficiaries were obviously family members and then friends; anyway, the

power was guaranteed to remain in the same circle (aristocracy).

After that first concession, and with the corresponding increase in population and human complexity, the concept of democracy was introduced
gradually: government for everyone and by everyone.
In fact, it is a concept that we have been defining for
over 2.000 years and it is not ready yet.

The current democracy presents a structural
contradiction: not all the members of society can
govern because they cannot come to an agreement.
This has to do with the variety of thought that fortunately is present in human beings. Thus, it is necessary to assign a few members of society to govern
through some institutions. A ruler, obviously, has
the compromise to govern according to society's interests and not pursuing his own benefit. But we
must take into account the conceptual tendencies
of political parties, that usually end up distancing
people from their needs even more.

Democracy, with all its advantages and flaws,
has been consolidated as the official government
form of the West. Its mechanisms are well known:
representative participation by means of elections
and referendums; political parties that polarise the
streams of thought; human rights and civil duties;
and the consolidation of the three branches of power: executive, legislative and judicial.

Despite the fact that one could say that the
current democracy is the most advanced form of

socio-political organisation that humans have implemented, we have to understand that it is a concept that must evolve parallel to the needs of our society. Today, we believe that we have encapsulated the essence of democracy, and that attaining it consists of implementing some mechanisms established and exemplified by some countries that call themselves developed.

No, we are still in the long road that leads to democracy. With all the advantages that we see today over more precarious forms of government, our democracy incurs in a small problem that has to be confronted in order to face the future without any social tension: there is a paternalism of the state, and a lack of responsibility of the individual by not taking charge of his own needs.

The paternalism of the state is the product of delegating responsibilities to an abstract entity, that does not have the same everyday needs as the individual, and that ends up generalising solutions. We have got used to demand from our governments the solutions to our problems, because it is easier to delegate responsibilities than to face them. On the other hand, governments, that are who concentrate power, end up getting tired of our weeping, tap our backs and conclude that the individual is just not capable of understanding the complexity of managing the fate of thousands or millions of citizens. From the tribune one can shout a lot, but on the stage, more than being complex, the situation is useless:

you can never have everybody happy. If we also add the ambition and cynicism characteristic of current politics, the result is governments that do not have the motivation to solve the problems of an apathetic and mediocre nation.

It is precisely those characteristics, which alienate us from our needs. It is easier to blame a government or a politician for our misery, than to roll up our shirts and get to work to leave our children a better world.

It seems to me that changing this lack of determination to fight is vital if we want to develop up to a space civilisation. The third world aid projects are based on economic transfers that always result in corruption, inefficiency or a waste of time, because their starting point is not the principle that to develop one does not need money but the will to progress.

Democracy, besides the small problem of the citizens not being responsible for our development, is threatened by the globalisation trend. This has a lethal impact because such process is guided exclusively by economic motivations. I do not want to judge human beings here, but the structure of the system that creates entities that have a life of their own.

Little by little multinationals and economic groups are starting to take over the state's role. This tendency ends up eroding the possible sincere bursts of social welfare by governments or their functionaries. If we continue the way we are, delegating the function of satisfying the nation's needs to the private sector will continue: education, health, infrastructure, utilities, security, raw materials production, etc. This warning materialises if we take into account the fact that the private sector does not depend on elections to survive.

The current democracy, that in a contradictory manner is attached to a capitalist economic system—if it is government by the people, why can people not choose a non-capitalist system?—has been questioned in vain by ideologies that go from anarchy to communism. The inefficiency of these proposals resides in them being theoretical proposals that failed to specify applicable policies.

In the case of communism—the greatest rival that the current democracy had—the mistake was separating individuals from power spots, without eradicating such power spots. The underlining idea was that no one had more power than the others, but that such spots continued to exist: the government, which after all is formed by individuals. The result of the communist game was to substitute the eternal power owners for new players. Same shit, different ass.

The opposition to the current system proposes a different power distribution, but it continues to talk about the same power. The solution is to end once and for all with the power game.

redefining concepts

The institutions in a typical democratic government are determined by some concepts that we must re-evaluate. Based on a new definition of these concepts we will be able to delineate the functions that the entities of a community should perform.

needs

The first concept to discuss is that of our needs, and how these relate to a socio-political organisation. Nowadays, the government bridges our needs and us. Our job, if we are as lucky as to have one, is only another variable to get what we need. The government provides us with rest of our needs. This relationship is affected by two attitudes: the individual's when he intends to abuse the system in order to obtain what he needs without doing anything, and the government's when it has no interest or motivation to satisfy the needs of the individual.

If our societies were not as complex, the individual would be held responsible for satisfying his own needs, but reality is different. The modern man, besides having survival needs, has comfort, artistic, sportive and intellectual needs. So we have to create community institutions that would be in charge of supplying these needs in a sectarian way, not a concentration of centralised power that delegates these functions. The difference between ministerial procedures and entities that directly involve the people is that the latter implies the participation of the population—here one must consider that the entities would operate at a community level, not national.

Nowadays, the responsibility of supplying some needs in the hands of the government is not an altruist act: we pay taxes to obtain those services. The neoliberal trend of privatising those services consists simply in changing the supplier, not the needs. So, we might as well just do it ourselves, with no intermediaries.

state

Leaving the development of a nation in the hands of a government is inefficient. The only way to supply our needs is to take control of our lives. We cannot delegate our responsibilities to an abstract entity that is far from our context.

The state's functions should be transferred totally to a community level. The existence of an omnipotent state is not a requirement to develop, it is a structural inefficiency of our organisation. With knowledge we can do everything we need, and that way we will not waste the human potential involved in bureaucracy, that after all does not produce anything.

By reducing us to a community level we could also leave aside the territorial concept of country, that has only been helpful to create wars and disputes. At a co-operative community level we could ease all kinds of conflicts if we implement an education of respect for others and we help each other by sharing information. This idea may sound chaotic or anarchic, but believe me, it is easier for neighbouring communities to come to an agreement than it is for two countries with several million inhabitants that have no direct contact with each other. Countries are only useful to create the identification that makes a football world cup exciting. If we are going to stick to nationalism, let it be for football's sake and only for that.

democracy

Democracy as we conceive it today is not really the government of the people. It is evident that the democratic machinery disturbs the functioning of a pure democracy: in any elections, the deal is not choosing between different policies that will affect our lives, but it is a competition for power where demagogy and theatrical arts fuse under a marketing strategy. How many resources—that could be invested in hospitals, education or entertainment—are spent in a presidential campaign?

Democracy reaches its highest expression when there is only one individual. But that is not the case. A true democracy is where everybody works in a sector that he likes in order to give something to his society. There is where he can really exercise his political life, when he takes decisions and actions that benefit his society. After obtaining our sustenance, there is something we can all do for our community.

When all these action sectors are aggregated—which number and function would depend on the needs and taste of each community—the political figure of community is obtained: a democratic organisation where everyone develops his talents.

This definition may standout for its simplicity, but I really think that organising ourselves in a community is not so complicated. There does not exist a single model, we just have to do what we like and do it right. The only requirement is that we teach our children to do things with love and using all their potential. In the end, democracy is more concerned with the daily manner of how we do things and how we relate to our peers, than with the terminology that describes the relation of an individual with an abstract state.

liberty

Liberty for a being that lives in a community is doing what he wants without screwing others. That's it.

It is not necessary to complicate ourselves looking for a more precise definition or some parameters to ground human behaviour—an executioner's job. The things that "hurt others" are cultural and evolve constantly; therefore, the struggle for liberty consists of teaching our children not to hurt others or nature, and to be considerate; that they are not the only ones or the most important here. And the best mechanism to guarantee this is to reinforce the idea of doing everything with love. I am really sorry if this sounds like a teddy bear, but that is liberty. The precious liberty is not concerned with what can be done, but with how it is done: that way all the things that can hurt others are discarded. The liberty of an individual in society is necessarily loving; otherwise we end up hurting others.

individualism

Individualism has two dimensions, and I think it is going the wrong way in both. On the one hand, our society is turning into a hysterical beehive where everyone lives for himself, without caring for others and with the only goal of satisfying his own ego. Feeling responsible for what we all do as a society is not relevant, and the best way of not confronting the shit-load around us is locking up ourselves in a bubble. If everyone goes his way, together we are not going anywhere. And to get far, to cross a million light years, we have to work together.

The second dimension of individualism is the one where imagination is developed, as well as the struggle of each one of us to find our own identity and to live according to our own perceptions. Our global society, fed by a tasteless television and under the telescopic view of market hunters, remains free of charges for the extermination of thought diversity. The exquisite peculiarity is an endangered species. If we all end up drinking Coca-Cola it is not as pathetic as if we all end up dreaming the same thing.

Directing our individualism is then vital to create a society where we all help each other in an altruistic way, at the same time that we take advantage of everyone's potential in order to improve the community in all aspects. Each member can do something, and it is a social duty to encourage those outbursts of creativity.

property

Property is another aspect that gives us an unnecessary insomnia, and it will continue to do so until we change our attitude. We still have not managed to shake off the "mine, mine" idea from when we were babies. We live in a race to own, to be the proprietors of everything that is around us. We have even patented ideas and parcelled the moon—which has been divided without consulting anybody and without even being there—in an attempt to make a personal profit out of everything.

We do not understand that nothing belongs to anybody: we live in a planet and we have to share the existing resources. The universe does not belong to anybody; nor any part of it. One of the biggest challenges for the future is to learn to give and share; to detach ourselves from the material things and to understand that the utility of things is the happiness that we derive from them, and not the things in themselves. Then, we do not loose anything if we share things so that others can be happy, too.

Accumulating only creates responsibilities that are an impediment to further enjoy life.

Defining a mechanism to substitute the concept of private property for that of collective is pretentious. The only way to attain that level of excellence is beginning by oneself. It is your duty to figure out what you have to do to escape the materialistic wave that is drowning us. After you free yourself you will be able to give others so that one day you may transmit it to them.

experts

The figure of "rulers" would have to be substituted for that of "experts." Defining expert as the person who guides—not orders—his peers in a topic of his domain. Counting on one individual to command an entire community results in corruption, abuse of power or jealousy; nothing productive. Then, a leader would be the one who pulls his people, not who pushes or commands.

A community has many aspects, and in each one of those it should have a group of people that guides the others. Such group should be formed by the experts and interested people in the sector. This way sincerity and knowledge are gained, and the most important requirement for a leader is guaranteed: that he loves what he does and for whom he does it.

community organisation

The fundamental principle for a socio-political restructuring is not to complicate ourselves too much. Do not complicate ourselves when formulating the theoretical basis or when implementing a structure. Politics is well known for mingling in rhetoric and not materialising anything that benefits people. Thus, we should simplify our socio-political structure, reduce it to a community level and attach it to concrete actions.

laws

The current legislative system is based in a constitution, and a law code—an encyclopaedia of all the possible crimes that is updated constantly. The idea, although noble by birth, has been proven to be inefficient at preventing the breaking of a society's behaviour code. But the legislative tradition is determined to perpetuate law production, ignoring the fact that the more laws there are, the easier it is to find ways to infringe them, and it is harder to guarantee that the population learns those laws.

Society should define constantly the activities that hurt it. But more than writing each one of them, it should teach the essence of what its members are willing to tolerate. A law code of 800 pages is neither fun, nor interesting, nor practical when educating the individual so that he lives in society.

Furthermore, those texts are written in a judicial slang not spoken by the people.

Increasing the production of laws contradicts the objective of such laws—that certain values of society are respected—because the dense legal weed ends up promoting the delinquents' creativity and does not cure the illness of our society.

After simplifying our laws and making sure that people know them, we would have to reform our judicial system. Judging has not coerced wrongdoers, who continue committing crimes. The objective is not to punish, but to stop people from hurting others. We would have to teach people to behave in society and not to hurt others. And this is a continuous task. If somebody breaks a law, we would have to show him what damage he caused and how he can act so that he does not do it again. This can be labelled idyllic, but I assure you that with patience and love one teaches the offender not to hurt society, or you bore him until he would not want to do it again. The requirement is that the entire society reacts when something against the law happens, and that they all teach the offender not to do the same offence again. Today, we only ask for the delinquent's head, but we do not aim to change the social context that makes it possible and appealing to infringe the norms: we have got used to put buckets but we do not fix the leaks. A judicial mechanism is not good for anything. One must not judge; one must heal, one must teach.

sectors

Each community should decide where it wants to get and define the activities that its members have to do to attain that objective. In this process, certain sectors or fields of action will come up and be backed by the innate interests of the individuals. Each sector should have an autonomy of action that does not hurt the other ones, and should be completely open to those who want to participate or get informed.

Defining an internal structure for these sectors is counterproductive, for that would depend on the context. A rigid and uniform scheme, established by a handful of intellectuals, is far away from the real needs of a community. Human interpersonal relations cannot be generalised. After each community defines the sectors required to supply its needs, each sector should find a way to operate so that it encourages solidarity and the development of the individual in order to satisfy the community's demand.

The way to evaluate the performance of these sectors would be the achievement of their objective. I talk about objectives because a community has specific needs, but the sectarian work is more a process that evolves everyday to achieve and maintain certain goals.

The relation of the sectors among themselves would develop in an atmosphere of informing, not presenting a report. Each sector should have its own dynamics and none would be considered more important than the others: the activities of all the members of a society are equally important.

Information would then be the key that will allow the members of a community to participate directly in its development. It is convenient to clarify that communications systems are so developed today that they can inform us perfectly. The problem in our society is the transparency with which that information is transmitted, and the people's apathy to find out what is going on. The vaccine for this is to simplify the language and develop more didactic forms to interact with the sectors.

Participation must not be focused to choose rulers, but to make everyday decisions; to choose between different actions. Whenever people talk without being concrete on what or how it would be done, it is because a personal interest is hidden. A mechanism to prevent these interests from filtrating is to talk clearly about the issues, and to discard the dull oratory that politicians use to persuade people—I am sure that they do not use that sincere tone when they address their mothers. If they use it with us it is because they believe we are stupid.

security

A sector that must take an urgent turn is that of defence. The modern state requires powerful armed forces to guarantee sovereignty and cohesion. Armies are for fighting, and while they continue to exist, there will always be wars.

A space civilisation is peaceful. But we are not. We have reached the despicable point of fearing a nuclear Armageddon: eliminating ourselves, something that so far no other species has managed to do. We are our own worst enemy. It takes acute imbecility to reach this point, and further imbecility not to react in unison to change such situation. I am not willing to legate the future generations a survival so fragile.

Then, neither armies nor weapons will exist. But the potential for reaction, organisation and discipline of those who love military life need not be spared. Such institutions should restructure to react in case of any emergency, and assist in matters of logistics and personnel for the construction of infrastructure. Also, it would be convenient to link them to research—especially in terms of civil and aerospacial engineering, and of nautical and all other marine sciences.

The advantages of such restructuring will be latent, but one can argue that it would create a vulnerable community. Such vulnerability must not be taken care of by an armed force.

The internal vulnerability in a community is overcome by the participation of all its members in activities that are needed. Dialogue is useless if everybody is not working in something that benefits his society. A spirit of peace and mediation should be taught at an early age. There will always be differences, so we have to learn to live with them without killing or inducing terror.

The vulnerability of an external threat is a factor that would be solved to the extent that we strengthen the links with our neighbouring communities. Cultural and sports exchanges, if backed by an information and knowledge exchange, are the most efficient way to strengthen the relation between neighbouring communities. It is smart to take advantage of modern communication systems to increase the reach of the communities with which we have contact. The larger our area of relations with other communities, the lesser the probabilities of an external conflict.

power anchors us

If in order to reform the economic system we must change money for work, to reform our socio-political organisation we must change power for love and the capacity to give to our community. The struggle for power that we have been carrying on our shoulders for millenniums does not let us take off.

In the measure that we detach ourselves from power, and create societies where it is not concentrated, we will understand that organising us collectively is not so complicated. If power causes conflicts, we must learn to take it in doses. Many organisms do it and do not incur the same chaos that we cause. Something so basic and daily as living together cannot defeat us.

If I come short in delineating some points in this chapter or you find it too ambiguous, it is because I am talking about human behaviour—as unpredictable as it is diverse. It will be in the experiment where one can document and define the mechanisms that will allow us to live in peace. I only know that it is possible, and that it is not necessary to wait another 1.000 years or for an encouraging prophesy to come true. It all lies within our hands, and what we accomplish will depend in our determination to triumph.

scientific and technological revision

Jose Rivera "Casado," a wise old man—one of those that you run into because life is generous or because it doesn't know what it's doing—told me one fine morning that all the inventions that we celebrate today were also invented by the Chinese 3.000 years ago. This slap on the face to our ego means that, despite the great technological advance of the West, ancient civilisations also bloomed scientifically although they had other perspectives and methods. And some of their fruits have not been surpassed by the West yet.

The Western Civilisation shows off its great scientific and technological development. Never before had human beings been so developed, we like to think. We have of course developed certain fields more than they had been developed before—just like we have left aside other paths of research—but this is due to the fact that we descend from ancient cultures. Competing with and having as a reference point the past is a narcissist and mediocre mechanism. Our reference point should be our imagination: What is more capable, our imagination or our wit? Until we understand that they are the same thing.

For the ecosystemic model described in the second chapter to be a viable alternative to the Western capitalist model, it is imperative that the new path offers a higher quality of life. Sciences and technologies have to be re-evaluated to supply better some of our needs.

a space civilisation

The image of a futuristic society much more advanced than ours, one that conquers space—and I venture to say that it is a consensus of what a good development is—is presented with large cities that house millions of people; sophisticated energy production forms; an industrial sector that covers the planet like an atmosphere; a giant transport system; food production highly technified; a frontal fight to control pollution with complicated artificial mechanisms; and a global society that breathes the highest technology...It is a society that travels and "conquers" space. This is just Hollywood. It is inefficient.

It is not necessary to complicate ourselves so much in order to obtain an adequate subsistence while we develop sciences and technologies. It is a matter of simplifying our society and channelling our energy into developing only what we need. A space civilisation is not industrialised and consumerist; it is nomad (or semi-nomad) and it adapts to the ecosystem, including the ecosystems of other planets.

The restriction of only using the resources present in an ecosystem will not hinder or make slower the development of our sciences and technologies. There is a way of getting everything we need from the ecosystem where we live; it is a matter of using our imagination. Also, a space civilisation has to learn to live—not only travel—in very different and/or reduced habitats. We must begin by doing it down here.

scientific motivation

Before revising the sciences—defining technology as applied science, from now on I will also refer to technologies when I talk about sciences—one must understand that these originate in one of the most beautiful gifts that humans have: curiosity. And it is just that deep inside we are more curious than cats.

This engine for discovering and understanding the world has three aspects that impulse it. The first one is that of auto-satisfaction; science for science's sake; science as a sedative to our tormenting and genetic obsession for understanding the universe. To this fixation there is nothing to revise; it is as passionate as art, and restricting it would be to castrate it—and castrating is ugly.

The second aspect is part of our survival instinct. It is to create a shortcut between our needs and us.

Here it is mandatory to revise science because it is time to acquire a greater efficiency. And remember that efficiency must be considered in terms of attaining our needs as well as respecting that other species attain theirs.

The third aspect deserves a section for its very own.

research and money

It deserves another section because we are going to talk about research and money. Absurd. Money should not determine sciences, but it does in the West. Ignorant. It is imperative that we free them.

Research is determined today by the available capital or the one it is going to generate. This condition is being as counterproductive to sciences as the religious restrictions were in Copernicus' time.

In a capitalist society everything costs, and research has become one of the most expensive activities in our society. Despite its unquestionable importance, nothing has been done to reduce its costs, and the state subsidies are being substituted more and more by those of the private sector.

Without money we can get rid of the pedant trend of patenting. Knowledge is a legacy of humanity, not a scientist's or a multinational's property. Without that obstacle and with a global information network, scientists all over the world will be able to work together and learn from each other. That is what science is all about. A scientist on his own will never be able to make a discovery, it is a group work shared from generation to generation. Our scientific knowledge began millions of years ago and never was the magic kingdom of science fenced by patents. We have to learn to share, to give. Patents are an egoist act rooted in the dependency that research has on money. Imagine that the person that discovered fire—perhaps the most useful invention in the entire history of mankind—also had the stupid idea of patenting it...

The unequal development within our species is not caused by the difference in capital between the South and North, but because the industrialised countries have a greater technological knowledge that they are not willing to share. This has obviously been allowed by the coprofagous and ass-licking attitude of the inhabitants of the South, that have underestimated their own knowledge and opted to continue biting the dust in the North's development road—it is convenient to clarify that there is North and South in all the countries, and it is vital to understand that I do not propose to protest or boycott, but to leave aside so much rhetoric and to materialise some initiatives.

We still do not understand that money is not power. Knowledge, thought and information are power. Therefore, to obtain a parallel development between the North and South, knowledge, thought and information must be shared. Free! As I said before, things are not made with money but with work. All we have to do is learn to work, to make things.

Sciences and technologies will benefit exponentially in a world without money and egoism because researches will have more information and freedom to research. Today, research is limited to those areas that promise an economic return or that do not present a patent restricting its access.

Money is to science as money is to sex.

scientific method

Western sciences, despite having attained great achievements, base all their information gathering process in a reductionist scientific method. Sciences stick to an inductive and deductive logical system, where there is no room for intuition or imagination, or at least not in a formal manner.

If it is true that Western logic has been a practical tool to systematise information, we should not assume that there is only one logic. Different cultures have used different logics to explain the phenomena around them, and each one of them has presented an advantage in a certain field. At this stage in our development, where a global society is consolidating, it is vital that we do not stick to one logic only. The diversity of thought is a tool that we must not bury.

This matrimony with logic discards the possibility of taking shortcuts to knowledge—that in the end is the objective. We soon forget that the majority of discoveries have been the product of intuition, imagination and accidents. Imagination is not only more important than knowledge, as Einstein said, it is also more important than logic.

Imagination and dreams—which only differ in the snoring—are reality. We think that dreams are the engine that makes life livable. This is the mirror of a tired and defeated mentality, without power or imagination. Logic is an abstraction of reality, a structured abstraction that does not represent the high probability of accidents, constant transformation and magic that exist in the universe. Properties that are reflected in dreams.

Dreams are the language of our brain—its operating system, so that the new generation understands. They are our perception of the universe. The voice that we hear inside our head is only a structured language of what ideas really are. An idea is not text; it is feelings, smell, colour, texture, taste, temperature, sound, essence, energy, love and the thousand more things that you may feel. Logic is only a way to understand the universe. To understand gravity one can use logic, but touch can also make you understand it. Science must go to bed with magic. The scientific and technological challenge around the corner will only be conquered if we let loose our imagination; that is power beyond our logic limits.

Then, with the decision of not limiting our sciences to the scientific method, and if we remember from childhood that not only nothing is impossible, but that everything is easy; we will have to restate sciences with the objective of attaining a development ecologically efficient.

It is also imperative to understand that sciences should not exclude each other. We have to integrate sciences, and to consider them as different perspectives that help us attain an objective, be it understanding or developing something.

the revision

Sciences will then be the joker that allows us to surpass the Western model. Now, one has to know in what it is viable that science searches for a manner to facilitate one's life, and in what it is not needed; in what nature offers us perfectly what we need. Science should not interfere with nature when its implications are very complicated and hazardous for Earth or for other species.

We should retake certain knowledge and practices of our ancestors (and some cultures that still exist today) that are efficient, do not hurt the ecosystem and do not require so much infrastructure.

Leaving aside the personal and passionate aspects of science for simplicity's sake, I will discuss the scientific revision as a survival tool that we have. In this task I will not discuss sciences separately; I will take certain fields of action in which a multi-disciplinary orientation of sciences should help us find an equilibrium between the ecosystem and our needs:

recovering the environment

The first thing on the agenda, I would say, is to clean the environment and to help in the recovery of ecosystems lost or damaged by our activities.

Putting Earth in shape means that we physically clean up all the garbage we have spread throughout our beautiful little planet, and we are going to do it with love. And if some technology is necessary, we are going to analyse carefully how we are going to apply it.

The ecosystemic benefit of this clean up is twofold (not counting the aesthetic factor): not all our garbage is biodegradable—it cannot be decomposed rapidly by fungus, bacteria and other organisms in charge of this job so important for Earth—and this causes an environmental degradation represented in extermination of organisms and impoverishment of the soil. Picking up our garbage will accelerate the ecosystemic regeneration to which we should aim at.

The second benefit is that it will allow us to recycle these materials to create new products without the need to extract new resources, which deteriorates the environment. If we recycle all the plastic that we have thrown away, most likely we will not need to produce new plastic in a 100 years. Here is where the technology in terms of recycling has to play an important role. The technological development of biodegradable materials—such as a new plastic that is already in the market—can help to incorporate the existing garbage to the new generation of ecological materials. Needless to say that from now on we should not produce any material that is not biodegradable.

The second stage, collaborating with the regeneration of ecosystems, is quite more delicate. This is something that Earth can do on her own if we leave her alone, but of course it will take several centuries to do so.

But there are two motivations to help a little bit. First, more than a guilt trip, it is the disgust for seeing the shit we have made. Second, that it would be an excellent exercise to one day install ourselves in a desert planet and having to create an artificial ecosystem, for example. Understanding ecosystems and their mechanisms is vital for a space civilisation.

We can speed up the ecosystemic regeneration process, so long as we do it according to Earth's mechanisms. Science—ecology, biology, botany, zoology, meteorology, agriculture and, overall, the indigenous environmental management practices around the world—must assist the ecosystemic expansion process without interfering with the biotic relations that exist among species of a given habitat. We should be careful not to introduce foreign species or genetically altered ones, because these can be counterproductive for others. If we see that our knowledge is not enough to understand the different ecosystems, it is better not to stand in the way and let nature act on its own.

The importance for us of recovering the ecosystems is that, according to the autosufficiency principle sketched in the second chapter, we will depend completely on what the ecosystem offers us. It is easy to have the intuition or to deduce that the more resources there are—more biodiversity and biomass—the easier it will be to produce all what we need.

agriculture

The current agricultural technology is based on three main pillars. Mechanics, with its heavy machinery and industrial systems of food processing. Chemistry, with fertilisers, fungicides, plaguicides and preservatives, among others. And biotechnology, genetically altering organisms so that they present characteristics that allow its production on a large scale. Although these technologies are efficient in terms of industrial production, they present certain externalities. Respectively: pollution and soil compacting; decrease of biodiversity, and water and soil poisoning; and genetic information transfer to other species in the ecosystem, without being able to predict its environmental impact. This is a quick glance.

All right, since the idea is to reduce the agricultural sector into small autosufficient nuclei, rejecting the current agricultural technology is not a matter of resentment but of being practical. Today's agriculture is just not viable if we apply it in a small scale.

An agricultural system on a community scale must be supported by knowledge and a precise technology. Being mandatory to compile the indigenous and farmer's agricultural knowledge, we must also investigate ancient civilisations' practices. Pre-Columbian cultures, for instance, developed agricultural technology—irrigation systems, terraces, green houses, selection and improvement of species, among others—that not having a negative ecological impact allowed them to survive.

If we combine this knowledge with modern technology we will be able to supply the entire world population without any problem. But it is necessary to adapt the current technology to a new agriculture, that will have two aspects: its small scale and an ecological orientation.

To produce our sustenance in these conditions, it is almost evident that monocultures—producing only one species in an area—will be left aside. These, the base of modern agriculture, impoverish the soil and imply a biodiversity reduction. Policulture, on the other hand, do not incur these inefficiencies, and they provide a more varied diet.

Talking about the type of technology that would be viable is premature before evaluating the characteristics of each ecosystem and the population that will feed from it. This will allow us to understand the functioning of the ecosystem where we live, so that we can determine the agricultural activities that will guarantee our demand. My intention now is not to define what technology we must use, but the direction that our agriculture should have: it does not deal with producing food, but in looking after a garden to take our food from it.

health

Health is a fundamental variable of the quality of life. Nevertheless, today's health sector is more part of the economy's dominion than that of science. Sadly, medicine has seized to be the art, the magic, of preserving the life of your peers. In a society without money, medical care of all its members will depend only on human resources, not on the economic status of each individual. The Western society prioritises health according to income; implying that the life of some is worth more than that of others. Now, that's a miserable attitude.

The solution to our health problems starts with an adequate prevention, that is based on a balanced diet, an optimal physical condition and a stable mental estate. Another factor that has a direct influence on health, and that science must confront is overpopulation. With a population of 6 billion (that by the year 2.050 is projected to reach 10 billion) it is obvious that we are an appetising and logical prey for virus—Darwin's example of rabbits and wolves.

Furthermore, a sanitary control for such a population is not easy to guarantee. We must plan a reduction of our population or wait for the crash.

If we manage to establish a prevention system that takes into account the former factors, we will reduce considerably the outburst of illnesses. From then on, science is a joker that we have in the evolution race. But as anything that is not natural, we must learn to use it properly. In the past centuries we have made science completely responsible for our survival. This generates a genetic weakness and deterioration in our adaptation capacity that could turn against us in the future. A real example is the exaggerated use of antibiotics, which has made bacteria more resistant, and we have to take larger doses all the time. Thus, it is wise to give medicine a measured and precise use.

Modern medicine is based on synthetic medicines and practices that require a high technological level; and it forbids traditional and/or alternative medicine practices. The use of natural medicines—whenever it is possible, and it usually is—seems to me more logical if we want to become a more ecological and genetically stronger species. Synthetic medicines may be very efficient, but at the same time they put the body's responses in the foreground. Today we see the trend of prescribing medicines at the first symptom, not letting our immune system or our body in general respond.

On the other hand, in the rush to hold a larger slice of the lucrative health market, we are not sharing information so that the technological practices of modern medicine can be available to the entire world.

Also, in some aspects we are denying other surgery and therapeutic paths just because they do not require a sophisticated technology—what we associate with better prognostics and treatments. Let us remember that before the second millennium BC, brain surgery was being practised in Peru, and much earlier in Europe.

Medicine, more than verifying the effectiveness of a scientific path or a conception of the body or illnesses, must deal with improving society's health. An to do that it must do whatever is required. If magic is necessary, then medicine must learn to do magic.

raw materials

Nowadays, a country (or a region) can specialise in the production of a raw material and exchange it for others that it needs. In an autosufficient system, engineering and natural sciences will be required to work together and develop further to produce all the resources required. It is to retake the alchemy that we discarded stupidly one day. In addition to that higher degree of difficulty, we would have to reduce the environmental impact of acquiring raw materials—which we are not doing properly.

There are three types of resources and acquiring each one of them requires a different technological application: renewable, non-renewable and synthetic.

The renewable resources are organic materials. These resources renew themselves constantly because they are organisms that reproduce themselves, and the management that we must give them consists of the management of their ecosystem. Resources such as wood must be not only taken but also processed in a more efficient way so that we can stretch its "life of use," and consequently, reduce the demand for such resources in the medium run.

Non-renewable resources, generally the minerals, present different problems. First, their extraction implies the construction of some infrastructure, and they produce a greater pollution in their extraction as well as in their processing. The environmental impact will be less when the objective is to supply a region only. But we will have to face the difficulty of producing them on a smaller scale. We will only achieve that by perfecting our engineering, and with a definite perforation of nanotechnology (miniature technological applications) and robotics into the current practices of non-renewable resources extraction. On the other hand and like its name suggests, these resources do not renew themselves at a proportional rate to the consumption we have been giving them. This implies that its use must be rationed according to availability in order to produce only the goods that are really necessary—not just to satisfy the caprices of a consumerist society. We must also implement a recycling system of those materials.

The third type of raw materials that we require are synthetic materials. These present serious environmental inconveniences both in producing and discarding them. Fortunately, in the past years we have advanced a lot in production techniques of those materials, and in making them biodegradable. We must continue developing these technologies.

To reduce the environmental impact of acquiring a raw material, we must make sure that the residue of its production can be used in the production of another raw material. Similarly, we must determine when and which materials to use according to the product that we need. A more sincere matrimony between engineering and industrial design cannot be postponed.

energy production

Human beings are not the only industrious species on the planet. But we differ from other species in that we have constructed societies that require an energy input superior to the one given by the food we eat. That is why one day we dominated fire and domesticated other animals—to include their energy in our life system.

Today, these sources of energy are insufficient to maintain our society and that is why we need to produce energy using different methods. We talk about an energy crisis because its production does not satisfy our demand. We even consider a symptom of development consuming a lot of energy. One more time, immaculate inefficiency.

In the last centuries we have invented energy production methods which have allowed an exponential increase in energy supply. However, they generate such pollution that the need for a change is evident. Not only the ecological movement and the civil society are aware of this, but also companies themselves, which are allocating efforts and capital to generate energy more efficiently in ecological terms. We are all guilty if the development of these technologies is not faster. We all are because we complain too much, but we all still maintain a lifestyle that requires exorbitant quantities of energy.

Now: a space civilisation cannot deny its energy demand, it has to face it and satisfy it with proper technology. Thus, the energy problem has two aspects that we must solve in a parallel way: producing energy more efficiently and decreasing our demand for it.

Up until a few decades ago, the energy supply was based exclusively on combustion systems, hydroelectric and nuclear plants. The former results in a decrease in the resources and air pollution; large scale hydroelectric has a negative environmental impact by changing flooding patterns; and nuclear plants present a high risk of radioactive pollution.

Of these practices, hydroelectric is the only one that can be rescued, and that is at a small scale and if the ecosystem's mechanisms are respected.

But we have also developed safer energy sources, such as solar, eolian (transforming the wind power into electricity) and thermal (taking advantage of the subsoil's high temperature). Although these methods produce less electricity, they are more benign for the environment—that must direct our energy production.

Parallel to the implementation of these methods we must develop other energy production methods. There is a very pretty source of energy that everybody has talked about but nobody has explored in depth yet, and it seems to me that it will be the mother of the future: gravity. Its charms are undeniable: it is present all over the planet, it is unlimited, it has a considerable constant intensity, and I have the intuition that its processing will not imply hazardous residue for the environment. Using gravity as a solution to our energy demand should not sound like fantasy; there must be at least one way to do it, and we are going to find it.

The other aspect of the energy problem is the reduction of our demand. We can achieve this if we ease our dependency on machines. Our own force (mechanical energy) can efficiently operate certain machines that we power with electricity today—yes, it is going back to Filingstone's technology. On the other hand, technology must sharpen to create appliances that consume less energy. The trend of making machines more compact must be encouraged.

transport

An economic system like the one proposed will imply a structural change in the existing transport systems. Since there will be no trade—which represents the majority of trips, fuel and infrastructure—transport will be reduced to tourism.

Transport directed to satisfy the human need for knowing the world is easier to structure than one impulsed by a commercial rush. Although speed will continue to be a variable when developing transport methods, we will be able to make more emphasis on security and environmental impact.

In order to optimise transport we must depart from the needs and then arrive to the transport methods that satisfies them best. For instance, for local transport it is more coherent to use horses, bicycles or vehicles that do not require fuel—even if at this moment of sacred ignorance we do not regard them as symptoms of development or elegance.

In the case of medium range distances, we must retake mediums that require little or no fuel—hot air balloons, sail ships, etc.—and reconstruct them using the new technologies in terms of materials, security and energy efficiency.

On the contrary, for long distances it is necessary to look for a considerable technological frogleap. The first thing to take into account is the fuel that we will be using because that will determine its ecological efficiency, and therefore, its viability. Once again, it seems to me that it is time to experiment with gravity. While that technological frog-leap takes place, I believe that there is no rush that justifies the use of transport methods that contaminate. Travelling is an objective in itself, and the final destination is not all that matters.

communications

The proposed society will depend exclusively on information to develop. Today, there are the resources to create a free information network; the problem resides in that we are not willing to share our knowledge with others. More than talking about a technological advance in the field of communications, we need to change our egoist attitude.

Once we have overcome that inconvenience, we will be able to use a medium such as the internet to exchange knowledge globally. More than refining the technology applied in the internet, we must be concerned with making sure that more people can access it. The communication mediums do not mean anything in themselves, what matters is the information exchanged. The final objective of communications is that everybody can exchange information for free and rapidly.

The communications technology challenge consists then in looking for a standard system of data transfer and net connection. Today we have developed software and components in the rush for taking the spots in a very lucrative market, but there has not been time to analyse if technologically we are going along the best path. The competition for internet has created powerful and sophisticated products, but perhaps it is more important to design first a medium accessible to everyone, from Indians in the Amazons to Eskimos in the North Pole. In this context it is evident that we must develop mediums that, metaphorically, would allow us to communicate manually.

urbanism and architecture

An obligatory topic to think over in order to reach an ecological efficiency is urbanism. The current concept of city that we are dealing with generates too many environmental externalities and ends up caging the individual in a rhythm of life that do not allow him to develop his own potential.

Cities such as Tokyo, Paris or New York—despite the fact that they represent our development and offer big opportunities—are not good places to live for those who are not on top of the economic pyramid: that is, the great majority. Problems such as traffic, crime, pollution, overcrowding and slavery to the life style offered by a city are suffered by millions of human beings; millions live trapped, used to the idea that the promise of success in the big city will never come true.

It is just logical to restructure our settlements. Although it is true that man is a social being, it is ridiculous to think that we do not cause any ecological damage when we conglomerate in cities of up to 25 million. Would you imagine a conglomeration of 8 million pigs—who are a superior mammal just like us—producing all kinds of residue in less than 600 km2? That is Bogotá, for instance.

The city of the future should definitely not have such a large population. It should be understood more organically, and therefore, its size should be determined by the ecosystem where it is located. A definite number cannot be fixed, but at a glance I would venture to say that half a million is more than enough.

On the other hand, the city will increase its extension, for it will be autosufficient. Our concept of city, hermetic and alienated from food production, is totally inefficient. Agriculture must amalgamate the city, break the rigid and artificial schemes of modern urbanism that end up alienating us from nature. The morphology of the city must be determined by an agricultural and ecological functionality, and not by commercial relations.

The urbanistic design as well as the architectural must reflect an ecological efficiency. Aqueduct, sewage and water treatment must integrate to create a more closed system where water can be recycled more. Garbage collection should allow absolute and immediate recycling. Finally, the management of space must be done in such a way that a thermal and energy efficiency can be attained, at the same time that we reduce our demand for materials.

In the majority of cases, modern architecture has stopped being art and become a line production business like any other. It is imperative to link architecture to aesthetics again. On the other hand, architecture would benefit greatly if it would integrate more with engineering. Despite the advances in terms of materials and calculations, for example, the quality of construction is worse all the time; one could almost label it as disposable.

Engineering has forgotten to investigate techniques used by ancient civilisations whose benefits are latent even today. A clear example is Inca engineering, still not surpassed nor understood by us. If we became extinct tomorrow, most likely in 200 years there will not be any architectural footprint of the West in a decent shape, because quality is not our priority. But the Inca construction most likely will still be standing in 200 years.

Finally, integrating architecture and urbanism, we should reconsider what living spaces need to be indoors: many living areas can be outdoors and collective—this way we reduce the area constructed. On the other hand, housing sites, streets, transport infrastructure, utilities' facilities, public buildings, production and distribution places, sports facilities, agriculture land, resources extraction sites and forest reserves must blend harmoniously into the ecosystem to make an organic city, diffusing the city's different areas into the landscape.

space voyages

Following the road that our aerospace technology is going, we are not going to go very far. I will elaborate: Alfa Centaur, the closest star to the sun is 4 light years away (4 years travelling at the speed of light, 300.000 km/s), and the centre of our galaxy, Milky Way, is at 33.000 light years. And this is just our little corner of the universe. To cover these distances, it is not enough to refine our infant aerospace technology, a technological frog-leap is required.

Today, spaceships are propelled by synthetic fuels, and they reach the laughable speed of 11 km/s. It is a dangerous, not very efficient and very slow technology: it takes us 10 months to reach Mars, the closest planet; and it would take us 109.000 years to arrive at Alfa Centaur and 900.000.000 to the centre of Milky Way—if we could take all the necessary fuel and were as imbecile as to risk sending a rocket with such an arsenal. The technology used by NASA, with all due respect, is worthless if we are talking about an intergalactic voyage.

Installing a base on the moon or another planet is proportionally pathetic. If we are not efficient here with our resources, energy consumption and residue control; we will not be able to survive for too long in space. And supplying the hypothetical base from here would be profoundly inefficient, costly and stupid. Thus, we must learn to live efficiently in the ecosystems of this planet—to which we have been adapted for millions of years—and then we will be able to live on other planets.

The former paragraphs were not meant to discourage space cadets, but to analyse the state of our aerospace technology and encourage us to search for other paths so that one day we can be a space civilisation. And we will be a space civilisation for the simple fact that knowing that there is an infinite universe out there, curiosity will not let us stay still.

But before anything we must feel the space. In the same manner that we learn to swim once we have lost the fear for water, we will be able to travel in space when we are no longer afraid of it, when we are able to feel it.

Space is not void, voids only exists in the heads of some humans. Space is an electromagnetic and gravitational tissue through which we have to learn to slide, and we must do it as energy, not as matter. The last words in the theory of particles point out that matter is just energy waves. Thus, we will have to develop a technology that transports or impulses energy at high velocities.

The distances to cover are so long that even at the speed of light they are unattainable. Thus, we will have to travel much faster than light, and the only thing that I know to be faster is thought. Although antigravity can be the first step to get off

Earth, I have the intuition that the technology that makes us travel in space will be very related to the mind. If the universe is an infinite life system, we will have to learn to interact with him at higher levels, levels that will allow us to play with his mental mechanisms to travel in space.

not afraid of jumping

In order to compete with the West, the sciences of an emerging civilisation have to develop irrevocably more than the Western ones. The development ideas proposed here will only prevail when we see that the West is not the most scientifically advanced path. And to attain a superior scientific development we must leave fear aside and trigger our imagination. If it is necessary to turn to magic—no matter how vetoed it is from the scientific circle—we will turn to it. The important thing is not to forget that there is no impossible. Perhaps at the "end" of our scientific development we will understand that the universe is what we want it to be.

Our sciences and technologies have to take a step forward; separate from industrialisation. Only when research is free—without any economic strings—only then it will find the way that is ecologically efficient, and pristine enough to jump into the scientific leagues of a space civilisation. I am talking of taking a trip in the universe!

evolution and education

Developing into a space civilisation requires an optimal management of resources; a sociopolitical organisation that promotes the individual's capacities; a technological frog-leap; and a strategic evolution of our species. The latter point is the subject of this chapter.

Our evolution as just another organism in this infinite universe full of life has been the product of the conditions present on this little planet. But I believe that our capacities in all aspects are infinite, and that we will even end up determining our evolution. We can only do this through education. We have genetic behaviours sculpted in us by ancestral knowledge—this is best understood by mothers, who know what mother instinct is—so we can also influence human behaviour and the physical evolution of man. Although it is a long run task, we have to begin teaching good things now, otherwise our descendants will learn the scum we do.

If all the universe is alive and we are just some cells in a playful planet, our evolutionary path to a space civilisation will be one of adaptation and integration with the ecosystems of the universe. Parallel to a physical strengthening, we must develop our mind in order to improve our communications, intellect and imagination. And most important of all: we cannot forget to galvanise everything with our love. Travelling through space cannot be so complicated, it just requires a bit of preparation.

conscious evolution

As we realise that we have unlimited capacities, we will realise that we can influence our evolution; we can set the direction, even if it changes in time. This direct communication between the genes and the organisms is only possible for species that have attained a certain level of physical and mental integration, otherwise it continues to be nature's business.

Human beings are a restless species that does not conform to simply surviving, but we also try to understand what is around us and discover the universe; we always sign our journey through the world. And if the idea is to travel in space, we can channel our evolution into that objective. Here I do not mean to manipulate our genetic code to isolate certain characteristics—and thus, in a way, end up accomplishing Hitler's dream of ethnic purity. Determining our evolution is not concerned with the how, but with where we want to get. All we have to do is aim and get in shape; nature's wise hand will write on our genetic code what it has to write.

Our evolution has two aspects: a physical and a mental one. In some areas they are the same thing or they juxtapose, but for simplicity's sake I will discuss them separately.

physical strengthening

Physically, we are an amazing organism: an animal, a superior mammal with a very complex nervous system connected to a big brain; we are omnivorous and have adapted to almost all the terrestrial ecosystems of the planet; and our complexion reflects an equilibrium between velocity, force and elasticity which makes us one of the most versatile organisms of the planet.

But these advantages are not enough in the fight for survival, and even less if we want to expand our action area in the universe. It is not enough to remain like we are, we must strengthen and develop further to one day be able to adapt to ecosystems very different from those on Earth.

There are two main tendencies in the West that are counterproductive for our physical evolution. The first one is our dependency on synthetic medicines. This addiction puts to sleep our immune system, and breaks the connection between the body and our will to heal. To strengthen our body we must begin from the inside, this will later reflect in our façade.

The second tendency is the lack of exercise that the body suffers. Our industrial and congested life style dedicates little time and space to exercise the body. We spend the greatest part of the day seated (at the desk, the bus, or the sofa in front of the TV), and few are those who dedicate time to do sports every day. We have to do sports daily and make the effort so that our society can have more professional athletes—imagine how many less criminals or hysterics we would have, for example.

Sports are a human activity as innate as it is beneficial; we should take them very seriously. A space civilisation enjoys an optimal physical condition; its members are strong and full of vitality—not pale, big-heads and asexual, how we use to imagine aliens. We have a body and we must strengthen it. Also, sports have a mental benefit, by improving thinking speed and intelligence, as well as working as an escape valve to all the shit we keep in our heads.

mental development

It is said that we only use 10% of our brain, what seems to me something rather arbitrary to say. But what I am completely convinced of is that the potential of the human mind is infinite. Developing our mind will represent important evolutionary advantages, we just have to make the resolution. If we decide to do it we will reach a higher integration of mind and body; perfection of our communication capacity; develop further our memory and reason skills; and will trigger imagination, our greatest virtue after love.

mind and body integration

Humans conceive the mind as something separate from the body. We do not understand that it is simply the echo of the millions of cells that form us, an abstract reflection of the effort that our components constantly make to keep us alive.

The adaptation capacity is perhaps the most important tool for an organism. If we reach a better integration between the body's needs and perceptions, and between our understanding of the habitat and our creative responses to it, we will adapt better to the medium. A very useful tool when we land on a planet completely different from Earth, for instance.

A closer relation between mind and body will also represent better health. Many illnesses and weaknesses are the result of ignoring the signals that our body sends us. Inexplicably, we forget that we have a body and that we must listen to it. Our mind is not autonomous and must proceed as the synthesis of the different parts of our bodies.

communications

A lot of time has passed since humans lived in herds. Now we are an animal that organises in numerous and complex social structures. This has been possible thanks to our capacity to communicate. But this capacity is far from an optimal level.

One just has to compare us with other organisms that live in great numbers, like bees, ants and some fish, among others. These animals have a much superior communication capacity which is evident in its organisation and lesser occurrence of conflicts and auto-destructive outbursts in their societies.

It seems wise to copy the telepathic abilities that some animals have. This should not sound like fantasy to you because telepathy exists in humans, and it is a matter of developing and generalising this form of communication. Its advantages in becoming a space civilisation are stunning.

First, we could substitute the helpful internet for this natural form that does not require infrastructure, is portable and that it would be free for all humans. In the case of a spaceship or a base, the telepathic immediateness will allow a precise communication that does not require a power source different to our body.

Another benefit is that it might be the first step to communicate with other life forms. This would be true for species that live with us, organisms from other planets, and with life forms of which we are part, such as Earth and Milky Way. This is a possibility that we cannot discard just because in this reductionist and anthropocentric phase it sounds ridiculous. We are talking about accessing forms of knowledge very different from ours, and we do not loose anything if we try.

Finally, telepathy could revolve our ethic and philosophical system. Telepathy could become a permanent information spider web—in a manner such as it happens with the millions of neurons in our brain—and it could function as a social control mechanism for those who hurt society: a collective mind that dictates morals, a natural and pure moral, lacking the limitations that we all have as individuals. We should not see this as a loss of individualism and freedom of thought. On the contrary, this would create an environment of transparency and sincerity where we would loose the fear of thinking differently, as we all do. Freedom of thought is not lost because it is public, and it is of little use if we do not exercise it.

While this occurs, if that is what we want, we can start by being open and frank in what we think, feel and say. Parallel to this, we should have an open mind: neither judge nor discriminate other forms of conceiving life. Perhaps this way we may put an end to the pretentious morality, and to the shame and guilt concepts that we have inherited. These have not coerced people from hurting society, but they have collaborated to control and judge the individual.

memory and reasoning

Memory and reasoning have been some fundamental tools in our evolution. Thanks to them we have managed to mold the medium around us in order to survive. What our physical characteristics have not been able to give us, we have got through our ingenuity. And in the fight for survival it weighs a lot to be resourceful. Here it is convenient to clarify that we are not the only organism that relies on these skills.

Memory has allowed us to accumulate information. Reason has allowed us to systematise it. And then, thanks to our imagination, we have created solutions that make our survival easier. But we must be aware that our memory and our reason have not reached their maximum expression; we cannot access all the information we have received or understand everything perfectly. Such information and its corresponding systematisation are within our heads, we just have to retake them.

Our concentration capacity and open-mindedness will be vital to trigger our memory and reasoning. Defining a method to attain this objective would sin of reductionism. The important thing is that we are aware of this necessity and that we dedicate time and effort to improve such abilities. If we learn to drive a car, why cannot we dedicate the time to improve our mental capacities?

imagination

The most outstanding peculiarity of humans is our imagination, our creativity. It is a virtue that has determined drastically our way of living. Because of imagination we arrive at some limits that in strict

terms of survival are unnecessary: we vaccine exqui-
sitely against monotony daily activities such as eating and copulating, and we explore infinite worlds of
personal expression through arts. That abundance
of creativity is what makes our lives extremely pleasurable, and we should never loose that. A world
without imagination would be like a garden without
flowers.

If it is true that memory and reason are important, they are useless without imagination. Thanks to
that capacity of creating universes within our mind,
we can come up with solutions to our survival and
development needs. The challenge of a technological
frog-leap in order to become a space civilisation can
only be confronted if we let imagination guide us.

Of all the mental developments proposed in this
section, expanding our imagination is the easiest to
attain, for it is an innate ability in us. We just have
to let our dreams flow; give wings to our fantasies
with the absolute certainty that they are real or that
they can be.

education

Nowadays, education is more a business in itself
than a vehicle for development and evolution. Government policies are defined to create a specialised
intellectual circle, and we put in the foreground the
average education of the population. A specialisation in all areas of knowledge is necessary to obtain

significant advances, but if the ground is too low the frog-leap will not be so high.

If we are ambitious in what we want to do, if we want to travel through the universe and live in peace, we have to educate ourselves. If we had an agricultural age, an industrial one and now a technological one, from here we should enter into an educational age. Education must be the main activity of our civilisation.

total education

Education must be democratised, it has to involve all the members of a community. We cannot waste the human potential by assigning to some individuals the making of some accessory functions, with the only goal of allowing others to dedicate themselves to develop economic, political, scientific, artistic or sportive fields. We can all contribute with something, and we are all going to do it.

To specialise more our areas of interest, we must have a more integral education. Today, the general studies, the superficial general culture, concludes with secondary studies—or at the most with the second year of university. That reflects a rather mediocre knowledge prism. There can never be too much education, we can never stop learning.

From a very early age education should give children a general introduction to all areas of knowledge—arts, sciences, mathematics, sports, humanities and languages relevant to the community—and introduce them to each division of those areas. This should occur during the first 10 years. After that, education would continue to deepen, but encouraging everyone's learning initiatives. We all have at least one field of interest, which should be promoted without leaving aside the other aspects of education.

A society centred on education also means that its members study permanently. It is not a matter of everyone getting a university degree and then just dedicating to producing something. Production must be impulsed by investigation; always looking for something to learn in what we do. It is ridiculous to think that education has an end, to believe that there is a level where we have learned enough.

The justification for a permanent education is rooted in our very nature: we have the world record for being the most useless and dependent organism at birth. And we remain in that state of supreme insufficiency until we are 3 or 4 years old.

Besides not being physically capable of surviving, we do not have the knowledge to do so. Parents are the first teachers. And that is a biological need in humans. But in this society, very early in the infancy of our children we retire, and delegate this activity of utmost importance to institutions that lack the innate motivation to educate the individual. The education of children in the hands of the parents should extend until adulthood. Only that in the West it is not possible because we are working to produce things that do not really mean a better education for our children or that they will return something to our community.

fun education

To generalise education it is necessary for people to be motivated to learn. Raising the standards of education implies that the entire society would dedicate to both studying and teaching. If we are not motivated we are not going to learn, because doing it implies a voracious curiosity, and only what seduces us pushes us. Thus, it is obligatory that we encourage children to continue being curious, and that the adults copy that gift.

Education should develop under a unique principle: education has to be fun. When we learn more is when we are kids, and we not only do it then because at that age we are physically more prepared to do so, but because we do it playing and experimenting—and we play all the time we are awake. From learning to add, to learning quantum physics, everything would be learned playing, having fun.

Theory and books should be documentation that teachers give to complement the games they teach. If the didactic material becomes an extracurricular activity, people will not see them as a punishment. Today, reading and researching are seen as tedious activities—not as fun stuff—because the educational method is based in a game of rewards or punishments for memorisation or performing a task. Pretty similar to the one used in dog schools: a biscuit for a trick.

pure education

Education must not be graded. Grades are not a way to evaluate someone's knowledge or capacities. They are a convenient way to reassure us that we are teaching: if somebody passes a subject it is because he learned—we like to think. The way to evaluate learning would be done in groups and would consist in the group attaining an objective that supplies a community's need, or that it presents research that is of interest to the group. The objective would be to learn, not to pass a subject.

The educator today is a landlord of knowledge, not the charismatic researcher that teaches not to resist the seduction of learning. The teacher figure has devaluated because the education system does not motivate to learn or work in a team—this only happens at very advanced levels of research, where there is generally money in between.

A faculty is too far from a table of alchemists, artists, Olympic athletes, intellectuals, medicine men, and other wisdom lunatics. The best of a society should be at the university—understanding university as the educational entity of a community, and each community should have its own university.

Education for a space civilisation is a way of living—even if this sounds like a slogan for a tampax ad.

love like a son-of-a-bitch

Everything I have said so far could be tumbled down with a finger. But what I am going to say now is the only truth, the only universal thing. And I am not the first one to say it, this has been preached from much earlier than Jesus and until much later than the "Love and Peace" movement of the sixties.

The only true and universal things are life and love. Life, because you and I are alive. Love, because then, how the hell is it that we feel love? Love cannot be justified, there is no explanation for its existence. Love simply is. And it occupies everything, like life does. Life is the only thing worth dying for—and for which we actually have to die. And love, on the other hand, just does not know death.

religious joy

If life and love are the only truth and are universal, these are god. God is not an anthropomorphic being that dedicates himself to take care of the centre of his creation: human beings. The idea of god will have to form a trilogy with life and love, if we do not want to loose such a divine concept: a private and exclusive god for our species.

A god implies idolatry, but life and love are not to be worshipped, but to be enjoyed. Now, I do not know if we are willing to reduce the concept of religion to pleasure. Goodness! This sounds like heresy, looks interesting, feels orgasmic, tastes like apple and smells like sin. When will we learn that even if there existed an exclusive god for our species, he would want us to be happy?

Life is pleasurable by definition. Life is designed to be enjoyed at every second. All that is essential in life, what we really need to do, is pleasurable: copulating, eating, sleeping, travelling, loving, learning, etc. Like any other organism, we are designed to enjoy.

the ego blinds us

Any human philosophy, any economic development, any power game and egocentrism, any human conflict or dispute; anything that is not life and love is a little shit. A cute and daring little shit, but the universe is much bigger, more inclusive, more relevant. We could explode this beautiful planet in a thousand pieces, but the universe would not stop. It is very occupied and happy creating life and giving love. The only way to stand out in the universe is to be the greatest exporter of life and love of the intergalactic market.

The modern man tries to extend his life, he wants more time. But time does not increase life, life can never be quantified. It increases when we enjoy it: enjoying life is to live more; and to live more one has to enjoy life more. The Western stress cancels out the benefit of increasing life expectancy. What do you need more time for, if you are not going to enjoy it? If you are going to be trapped in a traffic jam or in a job that you do not like?

All complications are of human origin. We have come to such an extreme that we have postulated the rejection of pleasure, and we have supplanted it with guilt. We should reject all these stupidities and enjoy life while it lasts.

the famous paradise

The afterlife is before your eyes. The earthly paradise, as its name indicates, refers to Earth. Earthly = Earth. Paradise = paradise. Why cannot we understand something so simple? We are alive, heaven is here, there is no need to wait for death to enjoy life...

The world is perfect: infinite stars and galaxies shine, they shine to invite us; there are plants, plants with flowers, flowers of a thousand fragrances; there are seas, lakes and rivers with a thousand fish, fish of a thousand colours; there are birds that live in the sky, a deep blue sky stained with little chubby clouds; there are millions of species, species that juxtapose with us; and there we are, with the capacity of giving a lot of love.

If we are going to expand in the universe, we have to turn this beautiful little planet in a little pearl that shines love—a little planet without love is like a kindergarten without children—and we must make sure that our space habitat is the most precious and flirtatious little shell in the universe.

justification for the title

The title of this book deserves an explanation. It deserves one because, among all the rhetoric that I have exposed, it is the only thing impossible for you and I to argue about.

Our lungs need air; our mouth, water; our stomach, food; our sex; another; our mind, information; and all our being, love like a son-of-a-bitch! "Son-of-a-bitch" being an adverb of quantity, and not a pejorative adjective.

Love like a son-of-a-bitch means a lot of love, an industrial love, a love that is implacable. Talking about love is not worth it, we have to feel it and make an effort to give more love all the time. A lame and idealist love is not going to get us out of the mud, we need a love decided to win, to make sure that there continues to be a playful and happy life.

Thought is power, and all what we think or imagine materialises in our lives. That is how one day we invented good and evil—that are not present in the universe—and now we have to live with them and with their havoc. The only way to get out of this counterproductive dimension is to think a world of love, a world out of the jurisdiction of god and satan. Love must rule over all our ideas and feelings, if we want to live in peace and develop to a level that has no precedents.

Thus, we need a power that changes the direction of our evolution. That is the power of being alive and living in a world of love—the mushroom power of which I talked in the introduction. We all have that power inside, and to take it out of your guts you do it by smiling. Yes, just smile. And then laugh.

Evolution and education should become part of love's dominion. They should aim at making us a loving species, one that spreads out in the universe leaving a powerful love track wherever it goes.

ecotek

I have left the dessert for the end. The experiment, ecotek, is thought to implement the ideas exposed here. But most likely some of them will have to be re-evaluated. I do not intend this book to be an academic document—which usually belong more to the dominion of a stool test than to that of human necessities—but an experimental proposal.

The condition for the experiment to work is that it would offer a better quality of life and a superior scientific development to the ones present in the West; while we live in peace, love and fun. The experiment will benefit the poor communities all over the world by paving a new development path, and by making it accessible for everyone. But the first world needs as much aid and guiding as the fourth world— it is imperative that we stop feeling pity for the poor countries; to progress one needs to work and not to weep: the only poverty that exists is mental—so we will share all the information and knowledge that comes out of the experiment.

Before giving more details I must clarify that the experiment does not intend to change the world. The world belongs to everyone, and trying to impose a way of thinking will sin of the arrogance that has accompanied us for so long. I only want to change my world. And if you help me and we create a better corner, perhaps we will transmit it to other communities. Changing the world into one full of peace, love and progress is accomplished by all humans; it is ridiculous to think that a few of us are going to do it. Thus, the idea is to create an oasis, a development alternative so that when we all get tired of licking the ass of a capitalist system, based in power nuclei, we will have a default plan.

ecotek

ecotek is a dream, a dream I wish us all to dream together to make it come true. The eighth wonder. It has been a long time since mankind made a wonder. ecotek will symbolise the beginning of a new civilisation. It will be a precious flower, a precious flower made with all the love in the world for some children that I am yet to have. And if you want to get something out of it, too, you can give the same thing to your children.

ecotek will be the most loving place on Earth. A place where the struggle for power that we see all over our Mother Earth does not exist. There, it will be a four year old girl, beautiful and playful, who dictates what to do. It is more than evident that the management of a human society is too much responsibility for an adult.

Thus, ecotek is a development experiment that being fun, peaceful and loving, would make us a space civilisation. ecotek is the name of a college town where the ideas discussed here would be implemented, as well as the ideas of those who are going to participate. The name only summarizes two characteristics: that it would be ecological and that it would imply a superior technological development. But the society that we will make will be a total society: a space civilisation.

university

ecotek will be a university that teaches, does research, and shares the information on all the activities required to subsist; all the fields of knowledge; all the fields of research that represent a greater development; and all the human expressions that keep us awake: arts, sports, etc.

Defining the structure of the faculties and the syllabus is premature at this moment. To do that I will need the support of a work team composed of people from all disciplines. What I do find necessary is to re-evaluate the current educational model so that the education at ecotek would be more integral, continuous, general and fun.

Integral education means a change in the concept of "career" that prevails today. An undergraduate degree will not refer to a specific discipline (for example, biology), but it will cover all the spectrum of the area (biology, chemistry, physics, genetics, anatomy, etc.). This is derived from the fact that things are more related among them than what we believe; a greater knowledge of all fields of knowledge arrive at a better understanding. We should expose children to all the available knowledge: believe me that it is not hazardous, and that most likely they can understand everything better than an adult.

A continued education also implies a radical change in the educational model. The existing separation among elementary, secondary, undergraduate, masters and doctoral education, only contributes to limit the individuals capacity. Knowledge will always be available for the individual, without even discriminating according to age. Continued education also eradicates the concept of graduation, that marks absurdly an end to the infinite process of learning. We will have to look for another way of rewarding effort.

ecotek will open its doors to everyone, independently of his academic background, with the only condition that everyone has to study and teach something continuously. The educational system of a space civilisation involves all members of a society. The hierarchical structure of knowledge incurs today in a waste of human potential.

Finally, the syllabus and teaching methodology of ecotek will be guided by an inexorable fun principle. To learn more we have to do it easily, and the best way to learn is to do it playing—by definition. We believe that there are things that cannot be learned or taught playing, but that mentality is the result of our pedagogy's apathy and mediocrity.

Education will be something empirical and practical, and as long as it is possible, it will be so outside the lab.

To develop into a space civilisation we have to find a far superior educational model than the current one. Perhaps some of the ideas exposed here seem to be taken out of a fairy tale, but we must project ourselves to one or two thousand years from now. Then we will be much more developed, and it will be the result of beginning today to educate ourselves, to get prepared.

The dream of becoming a space civilisation could be pretty close, although you probably think it is very distant. Most likely thousand of years passed before we could reproduce fire. But once we discovered how to do it, it turned into something daily and easy; something so simple that we still do not understand how come it took so long to discover. In like manner, an important technological frog-leap can be around the corner—it can be an accident or a lucky strike—we only have to be prepared in all aspects. We cannot afford to be unprepared to assimilate a powerful advance, as happened with nuclear energy.

city

ecotek will be a city planned to achieve an ecological efficiency; an urbanistic development that represents a better quality of life; and a superb display of architectonic design, very distant from the commercial orientation of current construction.

The design will be defined by those who work on the project. But it seems to me that copying certain aspects of the Inca architecture and engineering— that are not surpassed by modern architecture—and combining them with other styles and some modern materials, would give ecotek a construction quality that transcends time—like all things that are well done. After that, it is a matter of our imagination to make ecotek the eighth wonder. Literally.

The location of ecotek is not defined yet. The region of Darien, in Colombia, seems to me like a good candidate because it is abandoned by the government and it suffers the consequences of a violence yet to be confronted; it has a strategic position; it has enviable resources and landscape; and the most important of all, it is inhabited by very loving people. But it all depends on the different actors of the region, and that the government in turn does not start to complicate things or tries to play a patronizing role: the idea is to create a development path that omits the sociopolitical and economic structure that governments preach. If it cannot be in Colombia, any other place will do.

phases of the experiment

An experiment like the one proposed in this book requires careful planning, people interested in participating, and material and financial sponsorship. In order to satisfy these prerequisites, ecotek will be formed by different projects for each one of the aspects that would make the experiment possible, and those will form the different faculties of the university. Dividing the experiment is a way to avoid the formation of power knots inside it, while it facilitates the financing and supervision of each project.

Making ecotek will have four main phases. First, we have to get the people and the economic resources to begin, the Contacts Phase. After that comes the Planning Phase, where all the voids and ambiguities of this book will be solved. This phase will conclude with the presentation of the experiment, and that way get the resources for the next step. Then we arrive to the Construction and Set Up Phase: the end to rhetoric. Finally, we enter the Operations Phase, where we will work to achieve the essential objectives of the experiment, which will aim at creating a space civilisation based in peace and love.

project structure

Making ecotek will rely on a two-fold management because, on the one hand, it will be composed of different projects—this will be the way to interact with our sponsors/financers in the West in the beginning of the experiment—and on the other hand, all the objectives will aim to achieve the same development goal. This will be the internal management, where there will be no project of greater importance, but a symbiosis of them, working synchronised and in a complementary way.

Each project will have a specific objective that supplies a need of the community, while it produces information to be distributed to whoever is interested in the development of ecotek or in copying any of its practices.

people

The first step and the most important is to get the people who are willing to risk the Western lifestyle. Things, as I have said before, are not made with money but with work. It is us who are going to create an oasis, not money.

The main objective of this book is to seduce you. What I intend I cannot do on my own. We need to conform a group of determined and strong people that are not afraid of betting all to create a possibility of developing better. I am looking for dreamers and explorers.

It is not out of mediocrity or arrogance, but I will not accept criticisms to the ideas underlining ecotek—understanding criticism as a discourse that seeks to demonstrate that one is right, and that generally does not contribute anything to the one who is being criticised—I want you to complement them. The result of this book will be the work of many: this is just the beginning.

financing

In the beginning we have to get the financing for the Planning Phase. This will imply coming up with an estimate of the costs of having specialised personnel to plan each project, and of the infrastructure that they require. Most likely, planning will take several years and it is difficult to guess what resources will be needed, so funders will have to be aware of the difficulty of estimating a fixed cost for this phase.

Once the Planning Phase concludes, we will have precise information for what will be required to do the experiment. Then, the projects will be presented to get financing for each one of them. The costs of each project will include the infrastructure required for ecotek to begin functioning.

The idea is that financing will be done primarily by individuals from all over the world, not so much by institutions; this is to avoid political, economic and image strings. As long as it is possible, the contributions will be the things required, not money. That way we will reduce the inefficiency that all bureaucratic apparatus implies, and it will reinforce the idea that we progress more by sharing than by doing business.

After the personnel and equipment are transported to the chosen site, ecotek will detach absolutely from the world economy, and will begin to function in an autosufficient way. Here is where it will be demonstrated that surviving and developing without a capitalist economy is possible. From this point on we will be on our own. But believe me: all the other organism in this planet survive without money; we can, too.

projects

Now I will define each one of the projects. Each project will reflect a functioning need of ecotek, and will offer information to the whole world. Stipulating the requirements of each project would be premature, it will be in the Planning Phase where all the details will be specified.

I know that the following descriptions are ambiguous, but I do not want to be the one who defines everything. I need help. Therefore, the planning of each project will be updated constantly through the internet. Your collaboration in this process is welcome.

Without further due, the projects are:

planning

The planning project of ecotek will define each aspect that would make possible the experiment. This project will define and co-ordinate all the other projects; it will fill all the voids in this book; and will stipulate each step that we must take.

Here it would also be necessary to research all kinds of related initiatives taken in the past, and to contact those that are operating today.

Before we begin with the planning project it will be necessary to define what objectives and structure it will have. To do this I hope to count on the help of those who are interested. Now I only want to sketch it, here it is still raw.

localisation

One of the first steps is to define the place where ecotek will grow. The project of localisation will seek the collaboration of entities with information—geographic, biological, statistical, economic, historic, etc.—to choose the site that presents the most advantages.

ecosystem inventory

Once the location of ecotek has been determined, it will be necessary to make an inventory of the biodiversity, and a deep study of the ecosystem and the geological characteristics of the region. The objective of this project is to get the information that would enable us to install in the site causing the least possible impact, and to define the way to manage the existing resources in an efficient way.

After ecotek begins functioning, this project will be in charge of research in the field of natural sciences, and of the natural resources management.

economic transition

Depending on an external financing in the beginning, to then detach from the current economic system implies a study of how that transition will be done. This project will not only be in charge of managing the experiment accounts, but it will also plan the mechanisms to create an autonomous and autosufficient community.

construction

According to the management of resources insinuated in the second chapter, we should let Earth's ecosystems grow as naturally as possible. If I propose to built ecotek in the Darien jungle it is because its ecosystems not so influenced by the hand of man. That way we will be able to demonstrate that the best way to develop is to integrate with the ecosystems, not manipulating them so that they only serve man. Thus, it is imperative that the construction of ecotek is planned in such a way that it does not have any negative impact on the ecosystem. The construction project will be determined by the information gathered by the ecosystem inventory project.

The construction of ecotek has to be a master piece. In addition to planning an ecologically efficient city, we have to design a beautiful place. Aesthetics and functionality are a development symptom that we must follow. ecotek will reflect a fusion of engineering, architecture and ecosystem studies.

This project will plan the construction of the infrastructure, housing, university buildings, libraries, museums, restaurants, cafes, entertainment sites, services buildings, production centres, hotels, parks, sport facilities and everything else that is required.

utilities

In order to get installed in ecotek we will have to design the aqueduct, sewage and electricity utilities in such a way that the resources are managed optimally. This project will evaluate the needs that ecotek will have as it grows and develops technologically.

transport

The transport project will have to confront two vital aspects. The first one is to integrate an isolated community to the rest of the world. The idea of locating ecotek in an isolated place is to find a way to be absolutely autosufficient—although in the beginning financial support will be required. But ecotek must have an optimal contact with the outside world in order to facilitate the cultural exchange, so it will be practical if we locate it on the coast.

The second aspect is the determination to use transport methods that do not deteriorate the environment. Renouncing to those that do implies improving the ones that are not: hot air balloons, boats and sails.

communications

A main objective of ecotek is to share information, so an excellent communications system will be required. The communications project will define the required mediums to distribute and obtain information, taking into account that we must minimise infrastructure.

logistic force

What in the West is known as armed forces—that are in charge of getting involved in wars and maintaining order—will transform into an organisation that has the function of construction and response to any eventuality. The logistic force project will involve all members of the community, and will determine the structure and co-ordination that would make possible the construction and functioning of ecotek.

food

The food project will plan and be in charge of supplying the alimentary needs of ecotek. To do this, an integration with the ecosystem inventory project is necessary. This project will have to take into account the city's growth and will determine the optimal size of ecotek.

This project, of delicious importance, will not only be in charge of planning the food production, but in promoting the art of culinary. Nowadays, we suffer a nutritional deficiency that is not caused by the scarcity of resources but rather by ignorance.

production

To be autosufficient it is necessary to learn to extract all the resources that we need; and to produce the tools, utensils and machinery. This project will be in charge of evaluating what we need to produce, and how to do it in an efficient manner.

Developing a technology accessible to any community will be the objective of this project. A molds, plans and procedures bank will be created by the project, and it will be available to any community that requests them.

set up

This project will be in charge of defining and co-ordinating the procedure of installing ourselves in ecotek. It will make an evaluation of personnel and equipment transport to the site, and it will stipulate a time schedule.

education

Education in ecotek will function through interdisciplinary projects oriented to satisfy a need of the community, or to do research in a field of interest. More than talking about semesters or courses, it will teach the student all the necessary material to achieve an objective of the experiment.

The education project will define the educational model of ecotek: the objectives, faculties, curriculums, didactic material, etc.

health

ecotek will have a health system that starts with prevention, and that will cover the entire human population and all the organisms around us. It will research modern technologies as well as alternative practices.

sports

The area of sports will be of utmost importance, and the sports project will not only be oriented to teach the participants of the project all the sports that the ecosystem allows, but also to attain a competitive level of world standards.

arts

I am aware that I have not talked much about arts, but it's just that they imply a liberty that forbids defining its orientation. The only thing that I can say is that the arts project will encourage all participants to do art. If we are going to make the eighth wonder, we have to make sure that each detail is a jewel: from a spoon to a stadium, they are all going to be made with impetus.

ecotek has on its side the fact that we will not be determined nor motivated by economic incentives that prostitute art so much in the West.

documentation

Since one of the objectives of ecotek is to distribute all the information that we get, we will have a documentation project in charge of producing audiovisual material. This project will inform constantly on the development of the other projects. In this way we will assist the communities that wish to implement the advances of ecotek; it will explain how things are done.

Thus, this project includes all that a good production studio requires: cameras, sound recording equipment, recording and sound studios, etc. It will be the basis for the faculty of theatre and film—movies will also be made—but it will be integrated with all other faculties.

editorial

In a like manner, we will produce printed material that will be distributed through the internet. This project will consist of magazines and specialised books that give out the information on how to make things, and the current state of the different fields of knowledge; and it will be complemented by the documentation project.

Parallel to this, it will develop a printing technology that is ecological and viable at a community level—inks, printers, formats, etc.

It will also create a virtual library in the internet that includes all books and in all languages. The idea is to create an information system that would allow everyone to access the information wanted and print it in his own community.

cultural exchange

ecotek seeks a development path that would supplant the Western model that is generalised in the world today. By working only at a community level, it opposes the globalisation trend, that is deforesting cultural diversity. Being ecotek a university that seeks to be ranked amongst the best in a short period of time, it is necessary to involve people from all over the world. From the beginning ecotek will promote exchange programs with other universities, and it will open its doors to whoever is interested.

This project, working together with the transport project, will also have to make sure it offers the participants of ecotek the possibility to travel—this improves the cultural level and helps to share the knowledge produced in ecotek. A transport system that will allow us to travel constantly will be planned, at the same time we will establish housing treaties in the "outside world"—this is necessary because we will not have money.

aerospace

The aerospace project is justified as being a main objective of the experiment. This project will be a banner of ecotek—not the only one nor the most important—that we will have to take from the beginning.

human power

Before I talked metaphorically about the mushroom power, but what we really have to bring into action is the human power: our infinite power. We are all alive, we are all gods.

The challenge represented by ecotek is very big and the fight is tough, but, do you have something better to do? I am not willing to let the human species drown in its own shit, and let it stink Earth in the process. And to do that I need you to help me translate these ideas into actions easy to understand and to apply.

In order to create something perfect—because perfection exists—we do not have to sit and think, we have to be moving; and not from one side to the other, but doing what we are thinking. This means total dedication and conviction to ecotek.

By moving we gain momentum. We have to move our asses, and that means to do things with will. If we want to attain a superior development level, if we want to travel in space, we have to do it with balls. A weak and tired species never leaves its planet; the universe is for the powerful. Thinking that a saviour will come to solve everything is justifying our mediocrity and apathy, our lack of will to live and to fight. And that way we are not going anywhere.

There are two kinds of humans: those who invented god to ease their fear and the devil to install fear, and those who discovered fire to acquire power and comfort. What kind of human are you?

I cannot tell you how everything I propose will be done nor what the result is going to be. I know the road may present some complications. The only thing that I can guarantee you is that you will never see me kneeling and that I am willing to take it to the end. And if we consolidate a group with this mentality, nothing will stop us. Life is what we want it to be, all we have to do is live without fear.

We are going to create a powerful and humble generation; the most powerful generation that has ever existed. And we are going to make sure that our successors will surpass us easily. We are going to teach them to have courage, fantasy and lots of love.

If this book seems out of focus, too much fantasy, I say that we do not loose anything by trying. It is better to close your eyes and crash, than to open them and stay still.

16 years later...

In the summer of 1995, about six months after graduating from university, I thought of opening a cultural center. The idea was to create a space where curious and creative people could gather 24/7 to exchange ideas and produce something that would help mankind.

Without stopping to think how I would raise the funds, I continued developing the idea until it was clear that what I really had in mind was to set up a university. Once this was clear, my brain played a joke on me, once again, and the idea evolved into a college town. Since the idea was to revamp education, I thought it was appropriate to build the university in the controlled environment of a university campus, which in turn would be a small city.

Then, I began working for the COAMA Programme, a network of NGOs that supports the indigenous communities in the Colombian Amazon. There, I was able to learn about environmental issues and development projects—this had an impact on my idea once again. Since I was talking about building a college town, why not go for a full-sized green city? A city, with its larger scale, could answer the urbanistic challenge that developing countries face as their population increases.

In the beginning of 1997, I began writing this book and it was ready in the summer of 1998. I was 27 years old; the style of the book springs from the rebel spirit and the desire to "do something" that a young revolutionary doesn't know how to control. Being in a country where terrorists and criminals from all fronts made themselves be heard with bullets and bombs, I thought that only a raw book with a harsh language would make people listen. So, I gave away hundreds of printed copies of "Love Like a Son-of-a-bitch" and I distributed it for free on the Internet. The objective of the book was to spread the idea in order to find the people and the resources that would allow us to develop this sustainable development experiment.

In the beginning of 1999, I founded the Ecotek Foundation, whose purpose was to execute the experiment. The first step was to write the funding proposals for the international institutions that could be interested in participating in a development experiment of this magnitude. With a small group of friends we developed more the agriculture strategy, some urbanism concepts and the economic model. Meanwhile, I continued writing the funding proposals.

Little by little, it became clear that there were certain external complexities that affect this kind of projects. For instance, the international institutions would only be interested in financing projects if the government was willing to invest at least 50% of the capital needed. That was the only way for these institutions to protect their investment against a hypothetical government deciding in the future to cancel the project for political reasons—or for any other reason.

Then, the Colombian government was too busy fighting three communist guerilla groups, one paramilitary group, the abundant criminal groups in the country and the internal corruption, to sit and listen about a project that seemed to be taken out of a science fiction book. So, my proposal bounced from the mailrooms of the Ministry of Development to the Ministry of the Environment, to the Ministry of State, to the Ministry of Economy and to the Department of National Planning...

I was well aware that in Colombia you also need to ask for permission to the armed conflict players, so I began by contacting the theoretical branch of the FARC. After a couple of meetings, they recommend I forget about the project because in the country there was only going to be one revolution and it wasn't going to be mine—even if they had to silence me...

The last external complexity that affected the project—which coincided with the warning from the FARC and that I finally understood—was that, to be an altruist, you need to have power and money. I didn't have the former and I had just ran out the latter... I had no option but to use my last savings to dissolve the Ecotek Foundation.

I've never felt like I failed. The project is so ambitious that you would expect a "young man with no money and no connections" to end up crashing against the bureaucratic and financial reality—which in part is what I was trying to fight. However, from all that effort I learned many things, but the most important is that everything has its moment. Everything in the universe is possible as long as we find its point of support and we use the lever at the right moment.

When I signed the papers for the closure of the foundation, I knew that that attempt was not going to be the last. I had many things to learn and the right moment was yet to arrive. I was going to wait patiently until the time came.

Since then, I've been refining some concepts, and I've incorporated recent technological and social advances in my proposal. Regarding money, for instance, I have changed from the absolute abolition proposed in this book, to a multi-dimensional monetary system that guarantees the ecosystem's equilibrium, and that everyone in society can afford certain standards of quality of life. As I said earlier in this book, I don't want to be dogmatic, but to really build a green city that can show us an alternative development path. My tone has also changed. Those who know me would testify that I haven't matured much since then, but, as the years have passed, I have obviously gained more experience and knowledge.

Now, I feel like it is time to stretch and start preparing for the second half of this match. I've begun doing research again and organizing my notes to write another book introducing the experiment. This time, I will distill the bad words from the book, and I will focus on the execution of the project, from securing funding to the technical aspects of each project.

Books in English

Love Like a Son-of-a-bitch
Sustainable development

Escher's Castle
Novel

Sex & Modern Women
Self-help, relationships (co-author with Puki Bauer)

Finding Mr Right—Granted You´re Not a Bitch!
Self-help, relationships (co-author with Puki Bauer)

Keeping Mr Right—Granted He´s Not an Asshole!
Self-help, relationships (co-author with Puki Bauer)

DonJuanVargas.com

Books in Spanish

Un Poco de Jazz para tus Ojos
(A Little Bit of Jazz for your Eyes)
Compilation of short stories with graphics

Cariño como un Hijueputa (Love Like a
Son-of-a-bitch)
Sustainable development

Otto & Fritz
Novel

El Ladrón de Diamantes (The Diamond Thief)
Novel

Las Letras del Amor (The Writings of Love)
Novel

Homo Libertas
Novel

DonJuanVargas.com